EXPLORING KENYA

A CHEEKY SAFARI MEMOIR

RADA JONES

APOLODOR

Copyright © 2025 by Rada Jones

All rights reserved.

No part of this book may be reproduced in any form or by any electronic or mechanical means, including information storage and retrieval systems, without written permission from the author, except for the use of brief quotations in a book review.

CHAPTER 1
BUCKET LIST

THAT SWELTERING AFTERNOON IN THAILAND, I didn't set up to write my bucket list. I just ran out of excuses not to.

I'd just discovered that nothing focuses the mind on one's life better than a brush with death. Remembering that you're not immortal shoots a jolt of adrenaline through your routine and gets you off your assets. It awakens you to ideas you never considered and imparts new urgency to living in the moment.

Not that I needed it much. Looking back, there are few things that I regret not doing. That's because, come hell or high water, I did them all when given half a chance. But this was different. It was time to work on my bucket list. (If you've never seen the movie, you should. It features Morgan Freeman in great shape and Jack Nicholson playing a crazy man — how unusual. They both discover they have terminal cancer as they get thrown together by the vagaries of fate. They loathe each other, but to make the most of the time they have left, they decide to help each other go through their respective bucket lists. Believe it or not, it's hilarious.)

That's why one sunny afternoon, Steve and I sat to chat on the balcony of our condo in Northern Thailand — that's where we moved after selling our lovely home in New York State — to weigh our options. What should we do? What have we missed? What unmissable experiences eluded us, so it was time to do or die?

I say "we" because, as you probably already know, after a couple ends for any reason, life is not the same. Better maybe, but never the same.

So we sat to plan our future.

Move to another state? Another country? Another continent maybe? Been there, done that.

Write a book? A thriller? A series? A fantasy? A dog memoir? Seven of them? Done.

Experience life in the ER? On a cruise ship? Deliver a baby? Run a code? Check.

Climb the pyramids? See Stonehenge? See Dracula's castle? Are you kidding? I was almost born there.

Ride a horse? A mule? A camel? Been there, done that too. I would recommend sticking with horses and avoiding camels. They may look cute and fluffy, but they're shrewd, ornery creatures who like to spit and bite.

Throw a coin in Fontana Di Trevi? Marvel at Florence's David? Take a gondola for dinner? Fall in love with Italy? Done it over and over, and loved every second. Ditto with Sorrento and Pompeii. Same with Sicily, Sardinia, and Capri and just about every glorious corner of Italy. If you're curious, read *Driving Italy,* my last travel memoir.

Adopt a hedgehog? Plaster a chicken's broken leg? Foster cats? Pet seahorses and stingrays? Fly owls? Talk to penguins? All done. Not that the penguins listen. They're like a bunch of kindergartners on a sugar high, only less potty trained. They scream at each other at the top of their lungs while stealing little pebbles to build their nests. I've never addressed a rowdier bunch.

Eat lamb intestines? Roasted sheep's head? Snake soup? Grilled guinea pig? Fried crickets? Wood worms? Done that. The worm was a kind treat from a market lady in Laos that I couldn't refuse. Do not recommend. It haunted me for days. The guinea pig in Ecuador wasn't bad, but its disconcerting smile interfered with my appetite. I dropped a lettuce leaf on its head to cover it, but I still knew it was there. The snake was bland like chicken and so was the alligator. Only chewier. Maybe because they live a more active life. The tiny shrimps I was offered on my first trip to Thailand were barely larger than ants, but way too lively for my taste. Once hit with a squeeze of lime juice, they got all fussy. You had to swallow them quickly before they escaped. Given a choice, I'd go for the fried crickets. They're crispy and spicy, and they don't move. They also smile less.

That's why, after lots of heavy thinking, my bucket list was still mostly empty. Other than competing in a beauty pageant, which may be a bit late for me, training for a marathon, which is too much work, and flying into space, which is not my cup of tea, there wasn't much I fancied doing. Other than traveling, of course, which has been my vice for as long as I remember. Whether it's because of my reclusive childhood in the Communist Gulag, my ADD, or my wandering spirit, I'm not sure, but I can't stay in one place for long.

So travel it shall be. But where? I'd already seen just about every place I craved to see. We had recently returned from a long trip to Chile, where we drove from Santiago all the way to Peru and back, six thousand long miles, including some long days through the Atacama Desert, before embarking on a cruise through Antarctica. I've seen the Statue of Liberty, the Grand Canyon, Machu Picchu, Easter Island, China's Great Wall, the Kremlin, and Walmart. What else was left?

"How about going back to somewhere you've already been?" Steve asked. "Where would you like to return to?"

I thought long and hard. I'd like to go back everywhere — well, just about. I'd skip Moscow, Barbados, and Puerto Rico, but I wouldn't mind returning everywhere else. But there's no time.

"The two places I'd most love to return to are Japan and the Galapagos."

"OK," Steve said. "Let's do it."

We started planning, like we always do. We looked up cruises and hotels. We checked the average temperatures and rainfall in September, wondering if there's any difference between summer and winter in the Galapagos. Probably not, since they sit almost on the equator. We studied the flights, which were horrendously long and even more expensive, and wondered if the trip was worth it. After all, I can find turtles and seals on the internet, and look at fish at the supermarket. Much easier that way. Cheaper too.

Still, we decided to go for it.

But things got derailed, like they often do with us, and we ended up booking a safari in Kenya.

CHAPTER 2
ABOUT KENYA

KENYA? Why Kenya, you ask? Good question.

What do you know about Kenya? Not much, if you're anything like me. This is what I knew:

1. It's in Africa.
2. It has some of the best long-distance runners in the world.
3. It has wildlife.

When the idea of a safari caught root, I asked an old friend who's keen on safaris and has been on a few of them where to go.

"Namibia is fantastic, but awfully expensive. Tanzania is not bad, but if you want something great but still reasonable, try Kenya."

Kenya.

Like all modern humans seeking information, from the new mother struggling to stop her baby's hiccups to serial killers trying to cover their tracks, I went to Wikipedia, the repository of human knowledge. Trimmed down to bare bones, this is what she had to say. (Skip to the next chapter if these dry facts are not your thing.)

The Republic of Kenya is located in East Africa. With almost 48 million citizens in 2019, it's the 28th most populous country in the world. Nairobi is its capital. Its former capital and second largest city, Mombasa, is a port on the Indian Ocean. After being a German protectorate, a British Protectorate, and a British colony, Kenya became independent in 1963.

Kenya's neighbors are South Sudan, Ethiopia, Somalia, Uganda, Tanzania, and the Indian Ocean, and its geography ranges from the snow-capped Mount Kenya with its forests, wildlife, and agricultural regions to arid areas and deserts.

Kenya is a presidential republic where elected officials represent the people, and it belongs to the United Nations, the Commonwealth, and other international organizations. The gross national income of 1,840 million dollars makes it a lower-middle-income economy whose largest sector is agriculture. Its major crops are tea and coffee, and fresh flowers are its fastest-growing export.

Kenya's climate varies from tropical along the coast to temperate inland and arid in the north. The "long rains" occur from March to June, and the "short rains" from October to December, mostly in the evenings. The hottest weather is in February and March, and the coldest in July.

Experts say that climate change has led to long droughts, unpredictable rainfalls, and flooding, putting harvests at risk and creating favorable conditions for pest migration, and warn that further temperature rise might increase the frequency of extreme events.

But that's just the cold, boring stuff. To find out the interesting stuff that nobody tells you, read the next chapter, Kenya's surprises.

CHAPTER 3
KENYA'S SURPRISES

THESE ARE, in no particular order, a few things I found out after reading piles of books, watching tons of videos, and especially keeping my eyes wide open and asking our guide a million questions while there. I found them surprising, and you may too.

1. Kenyans belong to many tribes speaking over sixty languages, but everyone in Kenya speaks English. Most Kenyans are Christians and black. Other than tourists, I saw no white, Asian, or brown people in Kenya.
2. Ninety-five percent of the people working in hospitality are men. The drivers, rangers, porters, guides, waiters, housekeepers, and shopkeepers were all men. The few women I saw were managers.
3. It gets cold. I always thought of Africa as being hot, but it turns out I was mistaken. Kenya straddles the equator, but thanks to its high altitude, it can be freezing. The kind of cold that makes you wish for feather-filled comforters and hot water bottles.

4. Safaris keep to a rigorous schedule, and relaxing is rarely on it.
5. Plastic bags are outlawed, and disposable plastic bottles are forbidden in some national parks. We saw rangers confiscate tourists' water bottles before letting them in.
6. A Kenyan's average salary is $250/month, but prices and tips are American-sized. A night in one of our "tents" cost more than most Manhattan hotels, but offered fewer amenities. AC is nonexistent, Wi-Fi is rare, and power cuts are the norm.
7. Despite the countless cows, goats, and sheep grazing everywhere in Kenya, cheese is a rarity. We seldom found it on the menu, and when we did, it was imported.
8. While most gazelles, antelopes, and other herbivores are still doing well, the large carnivores are endangered. Despite extensive conservation efforts, the only predators still thriving are the hyenas.
9. Most hunts end in failure, so predators need lots of work, skill, and luck to get dinner. Even then, zebras and antelopes are seldom on the menu, and giraffes or buffaloes almost never. Hares, small gazelles, and baby warthogs are more likely, but they're not enough to feed a hungry family.
10. Relationships are complex in the savanna. It's way more complicated than "eat or get eaten." When they hunt, leopards hide their cubs in empty warthog holes to protect them from lions; zebras and wildebeests migrate together because there's safety in numbers; oxpeckers eat ticks off giraffes, rhinos, and hippos, in exchange for lunch and a ride. Elephants uproot trees and change the landscape,

but their poop feeds baboons, birds, and dung beetles, and spreads tree seeds to faraway places; warthogs stick around zebras and giraffes who, being taller, can spot danger sooner. By culling the sick animals, hyenas maintain the health of their herds.

11. Leopards, the loneliest, most elusive and stealthiest predators of the savanna, make an awful ruckus when they mate. The roars, snarls, and snorts of their lovemaking often attract hungry lions.
12. Most herbivores give birth during the rainy season to take advantage of the abundance of the food, but the predators have no season. So many cubs die young that females must reproduce again as soon as possible for the species to survive.
13. The cheetah, the savanna's fastest runner and finest hunter, has been tamed since ancient times. As witnessed by hieroglyphs, ancient Egyptians used to hunt with them, and poachers steal their cubs to sell them as pets to this day. But nobody has yet tamed the zebra.
14. No matter how luxurious the restaurant, water is never on the table If you want it, you order it and pay. As for ice, the only ice I saw in Kenya was on top of Kilimanjaro, and that's in Tanzania.
15. FMG, female genital mutilation, the practice of removing the young girls' clitoris, was outlawed in 2011. Still, more than one in five Kenyan women have undergone it, especially if they are poor, less educated, or Muslim. The procedure, which is usually performed with poor hygiene, often leads to infection, sexual and urinary dysfunction, and occasionally death.

16. Kenya is the world's #1 destination for female sex tourism. Mature women, mostly from Northern Europe, visit Kenya looking for a good time and companionship. They share their time and money with the "beach boys," young men who show them a good time in exchange for gifts, covered expenses, and occasional cash.
17. The Great Migration, the annual transit of two million wildebeests, zebras, and antelopes from Kenya's Maasai Mara to Tanzania's Serengeti is so massive one can see it from space.
18. The Maasai's traditional diet is keto, consisting of the milk, meat, and blood of their cattle.
19. Kenya's boomslang snake can fly between trees. It's venomous but reclusive and rarely met by humans.
20. Elephants use infrasound to communicate across long distances via low-frequency rumbles inaudible to humans.

CHAPTER 4
KENYA'S WILDLIFE

KENYA HAS considerable land areas devoted to wildlife, including the Masai Mara, where millions of blue wildebeest (which are not blue), many other bovids, and 200,000 zebras looking for greener pastures take a long yearly pilgrimage across the Mara River in the natural miracle known as the Great Migration.

I couldn't help but wonder who counted them all and remembered an old Romanian joke: A driver gets stuck waiting for a herd of sheep to cross the road. He asks the shepherd,

"How many sheep do you have?"

"359."

"Really? How do you know it so precisely?"

"I counted the legs and divided by four."

Kenya is home to all the "Big Five" game animals in Africa — lions, leopards, buffaloes, rhinos, and elephants — besides a multitude of other big and small mammals, reptiles, birds, and insects. Every year between June and September, the Great Migration sees two million wildebeest travel the two thousand long miles from Tanzania's Serengeti to Kenya's Masai Mara, but they are not alone. The many predators who regard them as their "all you can eat" buffet follow them, hunting the old and the weak, and culling their numbers.

This most extraordinary event feeds not only the animals — both prey and predators — but also the people. The local economy craves the foreign tourists and their dollars.

I can vouch for that. As soon as I googled "African Safari," I got flooded by an inordinate number of offers. Dozens of Facebook ads, emails, and even personal messages offered me the unique opportunity to book the very best African safari. Incontrovertible proof that my privacy was working. Not for me, for the vendors. Whenever you search the internet, be careful what you look for.

One would wonder how there can be so many best African safaris and not a single lousy one in the bunch. Whether in Tanzania, South Africa, Kenya, or Zimbabwe, they only offered me the very best. So, I thanked my lucky stars and tried to choose.

Not so fast, Sparky. The complications were only about to begin. What kind of safari did we want? By car, by plane, by balloon? How about horses? Private or in a group? How about lodging? Rustic or luxurious? Did we want to add a few days at the beach to snorkel, soak up the sun, and explore Mombasa's cultural treasures? How about a few days in Nairobi, Kenya's vibrant heart, to visit the Karen Blixen Museum, feed orphan baby elephants, and eat like hungry predators at the CARNIVORE, Nairobi's world-famous restaurant? How about chasing flamingoes at Lake Nakuru? A visit to a Masai or Samburu village to meet the famous warriors, learn about their lives, and enjoy a traditional dance?

The choices were so many I got overwhelmed even before we got to the essential question: When should we go?

The ideal time to see the Great Migration is from June to September. There's no rain, the weather is cooler, and with so many millions of animals on the move, you couldn't miss them if you tried. But that makes it more crowded and more expensive, and the timing wasn't great for us.

The second best is January. There's no migration, so the animals are fewer and farther between, but the vegetation is greener and lusher, and it's a good time to see newborn babies.

Few tourists are brave enough to go during the rainy season. It's greener and cheaper, and there are no crowds, but it's wet and muddy, and the mosquitos are ravenous.

Befuddled by choices, we did what millennials do, even though we're a tad older. A few tads, in fact. We searched the internet. Not TikTok — we're not that evolved. Just good old Google. Its sage advice, spelled-out in clear black on white, came from multiple sources:

"The best time to go on safari in Kenya is anytime between June and October. Travel in early September and you can almost guarantee that your trip will coincide with the famous wildebeest migration across the Masai Mara."

September it is then.

CHAPTER 5
THE RIGHT CHOICE

WHILE TRYING TO DECIDE, I stumbled upon a travel exchange that allowed us to request quotes from several agents. A few days later, we were inundated with offers, so many and so hard to compare that we couldn't make up our minds, so we flipped a coin.

Just kidding. We chose Right Choice Safari based upon their stellar reviews, which may be authentic. Or not. So, not that different from that coin flip.

But the guy at the other end of the line sounded legit. This was his first offer:

Jambo Rada,

Greetings from Kenya and thank you so much for placing this lovely safari request with us. Our adventure Senior Citizen Safaris are perfectly tailored to suit all travelers over 65 years of age.

Therefore, we have put together a variety of well selected senior citizen tours. These tours allow minimal road travel distances and incorporate air travel, ensuring safety and comfort while traveling along. This classic road safari covers Mara, Lake Nakuru, Amboseli, Tsavo west, and Tsavo east, some of the top national parks and game reserves in the country. It's an ideal trip for bush and beach experience. The wildlife safari part will take eight days, after which you will go to the Kenyan coast for an unwinding beach holiday experience. Safari starts in Nairobi and ends in Diani.

This is a private tour, exclusive transport arrangement from start to finish. The last day, we have a domestic flight from Diani back to Nairobi The said flight is carefully selected to arrive in Nairobi, preferably 3–4 hours before your outbound flight.

Meanwhile, down below, find our detailed itinerary for your guidelines and consideration.

This Safari Package Includes:

- Airport transfers on the arrival and departure dates

- Park entrance fees where applicable

- Service of a professional and experienced English-speaking driver guide

- Private transport based on well-maintained 4x4 Land cruiser JEEP with a pop-up roof for game viewing.

- Accommodation on full board arrangements (lunch, dinner, and breakfast) while on safari

- Game drives as per the itinerary

- Driver's allowances and park fees for the vehicle and driver

- Bottled mineral water during the safari — a bottle per person per day

- One-way flight from Mombasa to Nairobi, including taxes

- 03 nights beach experience based on HB arrangements while in Diani/Mombasa

- Airport drop off in Mombasa for your flight

- Government taxes

Optional Activities can be arranged at an additional cost, if desired:

- Balloon ride in Masai Mara, $430 per person
- Visit to a traditional Masai village, $20 per person
Package Does Not Include:
- International flights to and from Nairobi, Kenya
- Visa fees (where applicable)
- Such extras at the lodges/hotels as laundry services and drinks
- Tips and gratuities to the tour guides, waiters, and porters
- All expenses of personal nature
I trust the above guidelines will be of great help. In case you have more questions, please feel free and revert back to me.
Sincerely,
George

CHAPTER 6
PLAN CHANGE

THAT LOOKED GOOD, but not stellar. So we "reverted back" to George, as requested, and negotiated an itinerary that left out the seashore but spent at least two nights at every park we visited. Spending five hours a day in a car hoping to find a toilet before it got too late and changing beds every night was more than we felt like tackling. It took me a while, but I finally started recognizing my limitations and trying to work with my body rather than against it.

Just a few years ago we used to do Paris, London, or Madrid in three days and live to tell the tale. Orsay? Check. Sainte Chapelle? Check. Notre Dame? Check. Lunch at a cafe? But of course! Stop by the Orangery on the way back to the hotel and wake up early to catch the train to Giverny and return in time to see the Louvre before it closes. That was hard on the feet, but lots of fun. And fitting. We had to do it all in the few brief days of vacation.

But that is no longer the case. Growing old is not for the faint of heart. It comes with extra pounds, inexplicable pains and aches, and a perpetual need for glasses — I can't even eat without my glasses, let alone read. But it teaches you your limitations, those of your body and those of your mind. Some might call it surrender, but I choose to call it wisdom.

Growing old also gives you new freedoms. I'm no longer sweating bullets, worried I won't make it back for my next shift if the plane is late. No more kids to cart about, feed, and entertain. No more moody teenagers to fight with every day. No more elderly parents to worry about. And, sadly, no more fulltime pets.

Steve and I are both retired. He, from his water and wastewater consultancy business — his motto was "It may be sh@t to you, but for me it's my bread and butter." Me, from my career as an ER doc, not only in the ER but also on cruise ships all over the world. My motto, you ask? "Fighting Darwin, one patient at a time." Our son is all grown up, and our last dog, a German shepherd I named Guinness after the hero of one of my books, is now with him, and he shamelessly calls her Zuzu. Really! Is that a decent German shepherd's name? I wouldn't insult a Pomeranian like that! What's wrong with Valkyrie, Freya, Amazon (the fighter, not the store), or some other name brimming with force and majesty? Oh well. Sadly, after sixteen years with us, our beloved cat Paxil crossed the Rainbow Bridge to meet our other German shepherds and tell them we're on our way.

We now have time to do things at our own pace. We reverted to George, who turned out to be responsive and easy to work with.

Jambo Rada,

Thanks again for the quick revert and candid remarks.

I will remove the beach extension and make it a Kenya Adventure Safari package. You'll enjoy a seemingly endless array of wildlife, bird-life, amazing Landscapes with this 11-Day Kenya Safari Adventure. But it's not only wildlife encoun-

ters you'll experience while on this adventure Kenya safari — discover great cultures in Kenya, the Maasai tribe.

At a glance:

3 nights Masai mara (Mara Sopa lodge / Mara Simba lodge or Fig Tree Mara camp)

2 nights Lake Nakuru & Lake Naivasha (Lake Nakuru lodge or Lake Nakuru Sopa lodge)

2 nights Amboseli (Kibo safari camp / Kilima Amboseli Camp)

2 nights Tsavo West (Kilaguni Serena Safari lodge)

2 nights Tsavo East (Ashnil Aruba lodge or Voi Safari lodge)

I wasn't sure what he meant about the candid remarks, but everything else looked good. We researched the lodges, read the reviews, and googled the routes, trying to figure out where we'd find rest stops on the way. Finally, we told our family, i.e., our son and Guinness. Guinness agreed, like she always does — I've never met a more agreeable person wearing a fur coat. She never refuses a walk, never declines a treat, and she's a most supportive napping partner.

Our son — not so much. He rolled his eyes so far I worried they'd fall out and sighed that wary sigh he developed when he was five and I'd send him to make his bed or clean his room, as if the weight of the world crushed his shoulders. He's been practicing it throughout his teenage years, and he's got it even now, when we've lived apart almost as long as we lived together. Thankfully, these days he reserves it for my more unusual ideas, but after putting up with me for over thirty years, he's no longer getting in the way.

But this is far from being my craziest idea. There was that one time in Nepal when we had barely started tracking to Everest Base Camp and we got medevacked by helicopter. The six months of winter travels through Europe during Covid, when I found out as I was leaving that Americans aren't allowed to stay in Europe for over three months. The nice border agent was genuinely distraught to send an old lady to jail, even if she was a criminal. Thankfully, I remembered my European passport, which made me legal. She was delighted.

There was also that time I flew to Galapagos with a broken eardrum. My earplugs wouldn't stay put, so I snorkeled holding my ear with one hand while swimming and taking pictures with the other. My snorkeling companions took more pictures of me than of the fish. But that one doesn't count, since I never told our son. Anyhow, he rolled his eyes, and we started packing.

But, as usual, life got in the way. My body wouldn't cooperate, so September was a no-go. So was October, and by November we'd reached the rainy season.

After lots of reflection, we decided to try January. That gave me more time to recover. There may be fewer animals, but so what? How many do you need to get the idea? I'd be good with one or two of each, as long as they didn't eat me.

We had to rebook the itinerary and the flights, but it turned out that wherever you plan to go in September isn't necessarily where you should go in January. Things got complicated. We also skipped Nairobi, since we'd seen plenty of big cities and we'd rather see the animals in their natural habitat. We'll get straight to the bush business, we thought, and George, helpful as always, agreed:

Dear Rada,

This is good news. I am so happy you're doing well and ready to proceed with your safari in January 2024.

We thank God, and we can't wait to host you soon on our beautiful continent. I can see you have 13 days for safari starting from the airport on arrival and ending at the airport again on the last day, late evening. This 13 days expedition combines the thrill of exploring the most renowned game reserves and national parks in Kenya. At least this time you will have the opportunity to explore the northern parks and spend one night in the Ol Pejeta conservancy.

13 days—Chimpanzee Sanctuary / Rhino Sanctuary / Big five Safari in Kenya, best wildlife safari in Kenya

Safari summary

Day 1: Nairobi to Samburu National Reserve

Day 2: Samburu Game Reserve

Day 3: Samburu game reserve to Ol Pejeta conservancy, (Sweetwaters ranch)

Day 4: Sweetwaters Ranch to Lake Nakuru National park

Day 5: Lake Nakuru National Park to Masai Mara National Reserve

Day 6/7: Maasai Mara National reserve

Day 8: Masai Mara Game reserve to Lake Naivasha national park

Day 9: Lake Naivasha to Amboseli National park

Day 10: Amboseli Game park (full-day safari)

Day 11: Amboseli National Park to Tsavo West National park

Day 12: Tsavo West experience

Day 13: Tsavo West Game Park back to Nairobi.

Let me have your take on the new arrangements.

Sincerely,

George

That wasn't quite the trip we had planned. Tsavo East, which was — I suppose — East of Tsavo West, fell out of the itinerary, and Ol Pejeta, that I'd never heard about, was in. Why? Who knows? But adventure called, so we answered.

CHAPTER 7
GETTING READY

WE BOOKED THE ITINERARY, found some reasonable flights on Air Kenya, and started shopping. We bought guides and books to learn what to expect, light pants with cargo pockets that closed at the ankle to keep the heat in and the bugs out, and long-sleeved shirts that would protect us against mosquitos.

And that's where it gets interesting. Sadly, African mosquitos are much more than an itchy nuisance. Did you know that those miserable, puny, blood-thirsty vampires kill more humans than all of Africa's big five combined? By spreading diseases like malaria, dengue, West Nile, yellow fever, Zika, chikungunya, and lymphatic filariasis, mosquitos murder more people than any other creature in the world.

The best way to be safe is to avoid getting bit, but that may be easier said than done when your purpose is to explore the great outdoors. Still, wearing loose clothes with long sleeves and long pants sprayed with Permethrin, avoiding going out at dusk and using effective mosquito repellant on any patch of bare skin goes a long way to keep you out of trouble.

What we did may — or may not — work for you. Your best bet is to check out the CDC Recommendations on the web and speak to your doctor. We used Permethrin to spray our clothes, including our socks, hats, and shoes. It doesn't smell; it doesn't stain; it stays effective through up to six washes; and it's more comfortable to use than DEET, which I abhor. But I use it nevertheless, especially on my hands and face; 30–40 percent DEET works and is tolerable. One hundred percent is a darn poison, for insects and everyone else, so I wouldn't recommend it unless you're in a terrible place. DEET's new cousin, Picaridin, seems to also work well and may be less toxic. I like the Sawyer brand.

The second line of defense against mosquito-borne diseases is vaccines. The malaria vaccine is still a work in progress, and as of 2023, it was only approved for children. As for yellow fever, the CDC recommends immunizing against yellow fever but no boosters for those traveling to places with a high likelihood of disease. Kenya seems to be one, depending on where you go, but we fortunately had our yellow fever shots years ago, when we traveled to the Amazon. Still, depending on where you come from, you might need proof of yellow fever vaccination for your visa — see Steve's insert on visas at the end of this chapter.

The third line of defense is prophylaxis. For those who don't know, that's taking measures to prevent something before it happens. I'm talking malaria prophylaxis, which involves taking medications to prevent you from catching the disease even if you get bit. Thanks to the malaria bug's crafty life cycle that allows it to morph and hide, you'll need to take your antimalarial prophylaxis before you travel and continue taking it regularly during and after the exposure, possibly for weeks. The best place to find the up-to-date details is the CDC website, which details every type of prophylaxis recommended for the area you travel. Please beware, they are not the same. Plasmodium Falciparum that causes malaria in Kenya is largely immune to chloroquine, so the medications you might take to go to South America or Asia may not work in Africa.

I started us on doxycycline. It's an old antibiotic, but it still works on multiple malarial strains, and its most significant contraindications — pregnancy and early childhood — are not something we need to worry about. Doxycycline can also cause sun sensitivity, but we'll use sunscreen and we'll be covered. No shorts and tank tops for us. From a nearby DIY store, I acquired a hat like those Thai gardeners wear. Between the wide brim and the cloth that drops from it to cover my face and neck, I look like a burglar with a passion for beekeeping. I bet I'll get some interesting selfies. Between that and my clothes, I'll be more covered than a mummy.

To complete our medical kit, I got us Motrin and Tylenol for fevers, aches, and pains. Imodium for diarrhea, and a laxative, just in case. Also, antibiotics for traveler's diarrhea, decongestants, and our regular meds. The CDC recommends bringing a sterile suture kit to be used by a medical professional if needed, but I couldn't fathom carrying a suture kit to Africa, and the disposable ones are atrocious. And a sterile suture kit does not mean sterile suturing conditions. I ordered online some steri-strips to fix wounds, and I hoped for the best. Sometimes that's all you can do. Three years ago, I fell on Mount Vesuvius and got a gaping wound on my knee. That's the worst possible place, other than the elbow, because the skin stretches and pulls on the wound every time you bend it, making it almost impossible to heal without suturing. It needed stitches, but I fixed it with duct tape and honey, so the steri-strips should be an improvement. Sadly, I couldn't find water purification tablets in Thailand, but Amazon has them and they're cheap. Sports stores and your pharmacy may have them too. For the most informed and comprehensive health packing list, check the CDC.

We packed clothes, books, glasses, and electronics. Also, the new camera Steve will tell you about, our passports and copies of them (just in case) credit cards, and binoculars. I wanted to get some Kenyan shillings, but I couldn't find them anywhere in Thailand, so we'll have to make do. Hope to get some at the airport if I don't forget my credit card PIN.

I went to 7-11 to buy some moisturizer, and I happened on the superglue. In case you don't know, besides gluing broken stuff, superglue does a decent job of gluing together simple wounds when you have nothing better. Steve was delighted.

"Good. With that superglue and the steri-strips, you could do a heart transplant if necessary."

I sure hope it won't be necessary.

Finally, we had to pack our visas. Here's Steve's take on Kenya's eVisa:

Most nationalities require a visa to enter Kenya, but forty-some nationalities are exempt, including most of sub-Saharan Africa and a few others. Still, most western countries, including the USA, Canada, and European countries, require a visa.

Most western countries can use Kenya's electronic visa system (eVisa on eCitizen) but others, like Afghanistan, North Korea, and a dozen more require "Referred Visas," which may have to do with refugees or immigration status.

The Kenya eVisa procedure is more involved than some others, like Australia and Vietnam. First, you must register with the eCitizen site. This requires a recent passport-type photograph and entering all your personal information. After the eCitizen registration is granted, you can apply for the eVisa. All the personal information has to be reentered. Another photograph and pictures of the outside and inside of the passport are uploaded. These files cannot be larger than 300kb.

After uploading all the files a couple of times, you can pay *the $51 fee plus $5 processing charge. The website indicated an error with processing the fee, but it went through anyway.*

A couple of days later, you'll get an email with an approved eVisa attachment. They instruct you to carry a hard-copy color print of this document for travel. A copy on the phone is insufficient. This was a little inconvenient, since we were at a place without a printer, but we managed.

We handed the eVisa to the Kenya Airways check-in desk, but I'm not sure they looked at it. They did, however, at the passport control in Nairobi, and then again at our hotel check-in. They drew two lines through our eVisa and handed it back. We presented it again on exiting Kenya.

CHAPTER 8
FINAL PREPARATIONS

You'd think that after pondering this trip for months, postponing it, and starting again, we'd be ready with plenty of time to spare, wouldn't you?

You'd be mistaken.

Getting ready meant reading all sorts of books about Kenya — you wouldn't read them ahead of time, would you? Otherwise, you'd forget. But once you start reading, you remember everything you forgot, and it's often too late. Like spraying your clothes with Permethrin, which we postponed until we were ready to pack.

What's Permethrin, you ask? It's a wonderful invention that should be up there with sliced bread, aspirin, and the iPhone as one of the most wonderful human inventions. It's a substance used to spray your clothes to make them — and you — unappetizing to mosquitos. It has no odor, and, once sprayed, clothes look, feel, and smell (to you, not to mosquitoes) just like they did before you sprayed them. That's why you want to keep track of what you sprayed and what you didn't; otherwise, you can't tell them apart. It lasts through a few washes, enough to get you through a two-week safari when you do laundry every other night. Permethrin is not new — I first used it twenty years ago in Belize — and it's easy to find. Just walk into any sporting goods store like Dick's or EMS, or go online to Amazon. A large bottle that should spray everything you can carry is about $20 and comes with instructions and its own nozzle.

We brought some with us when we came, but it turns out that mosquitos aren't a big problem in Thai cities. The jungle is different, of course, but since we don't live in the jungle, the Permethrin waited in the bathroom for its time in the limelight.

When the time came to pack, I started spraying my khakis, bush shirts, sun hat, and socks, like I always do, but the bottle seemed to get lighter at an alarming rate. So, I skipped the last pair of pants and shirt to leave enough for Steve. I'll just wear the clothes more, I thought, and damn the smell. I bet the hyenas smell even worse, and I won't get close enough to the lions to matter.

A few minutes later, Steve emerged from the balcony with a sour face.

"That didn't take long," he said.

"Are you done already?"

"I'm not, but this is," he said, shaking the empty bottle.

His words fell like rocks, crushing my soul. I had used too much Permethrin, and I didn't leave enough for him. Now, if he gets bitten and then gets sick and then dies from malaria, it will all be on me. I'll be a widow and I won't be able to travel anymore, because lone elderly widows don't travel, do they? I'd have the entire bed to myself, of course, and I wouldn't have to fight him for the blanket, but all in all, it didn't seem worth it.

"Don't worry, we'll get more," I said. "I bet they have it here. They have everything."

And they do. If you're willing to pay, you can buy anything

in Thailand, from hair dye and Roquefort cheese to Dior perfume and gaming chairs that look like they belong on rocket ships, ejection included. You can even find the slightly creepy Jamon Iberico gracing the counters of most Spanish restaurants, stuck on its iron contraption with a long knife leaning on it like a violin's bow. It just costs more than a Honda. Compared to that, camping equipment should be easy.

Not Permethrin. I checked online at Lazada, Amazon's eastern equivalent. They had Sawyer's mosquito repellent and equipment for water purification, but not water purification tablets, and no Permethrin, unless it's for dogs or cows. And, even though I am fond of cows and cherish dogs, I wouldn't dare use their Permethrin, especially when the instructions are only in Thai, a language I can't understand and even less read. Have you ever seen Thai writing? It's a jolly congregation of lively wiggles who seem to have an excellent time, but they bear no resemblance to any alphabet I'm familiar with. Not Roman, not Greek, and not even Cyrillic.

Even worse, unlike any other language I know, Thai is a tonal language, so a word's meaning comes from its tone. Take, for example, the word MAI. Depending on how you say it, it means: 1. No. 2. New. 3. Burned. 4. Wood. 5. Silk. 6. Yarn. And I bet there are more. I've been studying Thai for a year with the nicest teacher, but I still don't know enough to buy aspirin, let alone buy Permethrin for cows and use it without endangering my marriage. Not even Google Translate works for Thai, unless you're looking to have a good laugh.

Back to Permethrin. I checked with Mr. Google, located the nearest sports store, then loaded Steve into one of the open trucks they call Tuk-Tuks, used here as public transportation, and went to look for Permethrin.

Explaining to the Thai vendors at the North Face what I needed was a challenge. It involved all my limbs and a multitude of facial expressions, but I somehow conveyed that I needed a spray. What kind of spray? That was harder, but after I buzzed like a mosquito and slapped myself silly, they sent me to the pharmacy.

I wasn't sure if it was for a mosquito spray or a sedative, but who was I to disagree? Much to the delight of the shoppers gathered to watch, I performed the same pantomime at Watsons, Boots, and a few other drugstores in the mall. Sharp as usual, the Thai vendors understood what I needed. Almost. They offered me plug-in mosquito deterrents, smoking coils, citronella, lemon grass candles, and a variety of sun protection. All useful, but nothing that would make Steve's clothes mosquito proof. One particularly astute lady suggested something to fumigate rooms against all living beings, but I decided against it. For now.

I gave up. With a heavy heart, I ordered Permethrin on Amazon and had it shipped to our son (they don't ship it to Thailand, and neither does Dick's or EMS.) I asked him to send it here. But it's just after Christmas, the world is ablaze with wars, and the Houthi rebels have throttled the passage from the Gulf of Aden to the Red Sea, playing havoc with the world's shipping, so it's not likely our Permethrin will arrive in time. But there's nothing else I can do. I hope Steve makes it.

CHAPTER 9
STEVE'S TAKE ON THE CAMERA AND ELECTRONICS

We travel a lot, but we're not brilliant photographers. Still, for the safari, we wanted a camera with better magnification than an iPhone, but not one of those large single-lens reflex cameras with bulky interchangeable lenses. Years ago, we took a Canon EOS DSLR to Machu Picchu, Galapagos, Easter Island, and a few other adventures. It was too bulky, it never had the right lens installed for the photo-op, and we rarely had it with us when we wanted it.

Following the adage that the best camera is the one you have with you, we sold the DSLR and documented our voyages with iPhones. But as we planned for the safari, we doubted the wild game would come close enough for an iPhone picture and began looking for a better alternative.

We wanted a travel camera with at least 20X magnification. That's roughly equivalent to about a 500mm lens on an SLR, and about the limit for a handheld camera.

So we began the quest for the right travel camera. Our friends have a Nikon Coolpix zoom with a fantastic 83X magnification (2000mm equivalent), but it weighs almost 3 pounds and is as large as the SLR we sold. That makes it almost impos-

sible to use the higher magnification without a tripod because of the "jitter."

I spent many hours investigating and reading review articles, but every camera I tried to purchase turned out to be used or "refurbished," but still more expensive than the new ones. I couldn't find a new one from Amazon, nor from my old standby source, B&H Photo in NYC. All the major manufacturers had discontinued their zoom travel cameras. Maybe because they're not good for selfies?

Our location in Thailand complicated delivery even further.

In desperation, I turned to eBay, even though I didn't want a used camera. After searching all the better reviewed models, I found a camera store in Italy advertising a NEW Canon SX740 HS with 40X optical zoom, and I ordered it. I requested expedited delivery in English, but I got a nonspecific response in Italian. Still, FedEx delivered it in just a few days. The store had filled out a customs declaration, and we paid a 7 percent Thailand import duty to the delivery driver.

I ordered extra batteries, memory cards, and a mobile charger from Lazada, our local version of Amazon. They arrived a few days later. Canon brand batteries cost three times more than off-brand, but I had previous bad experiences with cameras rejecting off-brand batteries. We also needed higher speed SD cards, and I opted for multiple smaller cards instead of a single high-capacity card that might crash and lose everything.

The camera worked properly, which was a relief, since returning it would be a nightmare. If anything, it has too many features, with auto-focusing, focus tracking, scene recognition, facial recognition, video modes, etc. The 40X magnification is equivalent to a 960 mm lens on an old 35mm. You've probably seen professionals with these monsters. They're so massive that the tripod holds the lens while the camera hangs off the back.

So far, I've found the 40X to be pretty much useless without a tripod. Just depressing the shutter moves the subject out of the frame, if you can find the subject at all. But with the lens retracted, the camera is small enough to fit into a pocket. That's a plus.

LATER NOTE:

The camera was difficult to control during the safari. It was almost impossible to focus when the vehicle was moving, even when zoomed out all the way. When we stopped, I had to be careful not to lean against the vehicle because of engine vibrations. When our driver turned off the engine for the better photo ops, I leaned against the vehicle and used the full zoom capability. About half the photos were blurred, or the subject was out of the frame, but some were excellent.

We took about two hundred pictures and a couple of videos every day and downloaded them to the MacBook in the evening using the SD memory card adapter. But one evening the card adapter failed, and my repeated attempts to upload with the broken adapter corrupted the memory card.

The next morning I loaded a fresh memory card and asked our guide Francis to find us an electronics store to purchase a new adapter. We stopped in the largest town on the way, but three different shops had no adapters. Fortunately, I could connect directly to the camera with the interface cable I had brought.

Our laptop, however, failed to recognize the camera. I spent a lot of time troubleshooting on the internet in the camp common area, the only place with Wi-Fi. Apparently, the new updates of the Mac operating system were incompatible with the camera since Canon was several systems behind with publishing fixes, so we couldn't use a direct connection to upload our photos. Fortunately, I had brought enough memory cards for the remaining days of the safari.

After returning home, I tried our old backup Mac. It connected to the camera instantly, allowing me to upload all the remaining photos. Not sure why it worked, maybe because it had an older operating system? Anyway, I got the photos in our iCloud storage, and they are magnificent.

Electronics

Kenya, a former British Protectorate, has 220-Volt grid power and uses all UK Type G receptacles. These receptacles use very large plugs that require adapters for almost all chargers. We found a large universal adapter at a DIY store in Thailand that converted from UK receptacles to European and US plugs, and included two USB outlets.

The camera sourced from Italy came with an OEM European charger that we left home in favor of an aftermarket dual USB charger. We brought a 65-Watt USB Type-C charger for both laptops and phones and also a cigarette lighter charger and a 95Watthour power bank to use in the vehicle. That was a lifesaver for our iPhones.

Setting up all this equipment in every tent was a little inconvenient, but we never ran out of battery power.

CHAPTER 10
THE SAFARI JACKET

As we prepared for the safari, we were in Jomtien, a seaside resort in southern Thailand. We had booked our flights from Bangkok, about two hours' drive away, but we had no car, so we'd have to find a way to get to the airport.

That shouldn't be hard, I thought. The Beach Road, Jomtien's main street, was nothing but restaurants, shops, and massage parlors covered with posters advertising transport to the Bangkok airport. Depending on our wallet and inclination, we could share a minibus with a dozen new close friends, take a private taxi or a limo, or take the bus. The taxi prices were all over the place, from 1400 to 2000 baht — about $60. Not much for a two-hour drive, but not knowing whether someone would actually show up or we'd be sitting on our luggage while our plane took off made for an uncomfortable proposition. We decided on the bus. It has a fixed schedule, and it's air-conditioned and dirt cheap — about $10 for us both, luggage included.

I felt pretty proud of myself for booking the trip for the right date and in the correct direction, despite the Thai-only instructions. Our son had shipped the Permethrin, so maybe we'd get it in time. Life looked pretty good after all, so I decided to start packing.

But, as I often do when tackling a non-exciting task, I started with a break. I sat in my sun chair on the balcony to watch people baking themselves by the pool and checked my laptop for the news.

That's when I saw Mariska Hargitay. She's a famous American actress with a loyal following. Just days before our departure, she was on a safari in Kenya, socializing with a haughty giraffe who looked down at her. Literally. Those giraffes must be damn tall.

Not bad, I thought, until I examined them closer.

The giraffe looked just fine. She sported the usual markings, a long neck, and a cute pair of ossicones — the snail-like little horns giraffes love to wear. She seemed amused, as if someone had told her a joke.

Mariska looked happy and posh in her safari jacket, with a flowing scarf around her neck, a pair of tan cargo pants so well pressed they could draw blood, and a blissful smile.

Wait, what? Well-pressed pants? Do you need those in the savanna? Do the giraffes even care?

And a safari jacket? Isn't it supposed to be hot? Like boiling hot? Isn't it always hot in Africa? That's what I'd thought, so other than my trusted old raincoat, I only had a few ultra-light, quick-drying SPF-enhanced hiking shirts sprayed with Permethrin, besides my socks and underwear.

I enlarged the picture to count the layers.

Yep, safari jacket it was, zipped up, over a textured cotton sweater, on top of a safari shirt, over a t-shirt and who knows what else, besides the pearls and the scarf.

Not good.

In another picture, she'd even wrapped one of those red

Masai blankets around her, and she didn't look like she was sweating.

Darn.

Where do I find a safari jacket? And what was I thinking, not looking for one months ago?

I went back to Lazada, Amazon's Eastern equivalent, where one can find everything. Other than Permethrin and water purifying tablets, that is.

My search for safari jackets resulted in a fake camel-hair coat, a quilted jacket sprinkled with unicorns, and a lacy see-through garment with leopard spots meant to showcase the charms of the wearer. Giraffes would love that, I thought. Mosquitos would love it even more.

Amazon had something closer, but it was too late to get it shipped. The only thing left to do was to go shopping.

I dragged Steve out to the mall with the promise of buying him lunch. Not any lunch, mind you, but a Farang lunch. In Thailand, the term Farang refers to Westerners, whether they're American, Australian, French or German. Farang food, therefore, is pretty much any food that is not Thai, Chinese, or Indian.

That got his attention. Steve tolerates some Thai dishes, especially Pad Thai and fried chicken with lime leaves, but he doesn't care for spicy food. Moreover, he craves the food he grew up with. His comfort foods are burgers, pizza, and steak, not Som-Tum (green papaya salad with hot peppers,) Tom-Young-Goong (hot-and spicy shrimp soup with mushrooms) or Larb (a ground meat salad so spicy it makes you cry.)

For about half a dollar, the baht bus, a low open truck with two long benches in the back, took us all the way to Terminal 21, Pattaya's newest mall. We expected to see a mall like any other, but it wasn't. Terminal 21 was a traveler's dream turned mall.

"Whoever built this did a good job," Steve said, gawking at the mall's peculiar design. From the murals, statues, and decorations to the toilets, every one of Terminal 21's floors resembles a different destination. The ground floor wraps around a three-floor high Eiffel Tower and showcases the Parisian metro and a French bakery. The first floor is nothing but red phone booths, double-decker buses, and English boobies. The third floor centers on an impressive Leaning Tower of Pisa and sports full-sized gondolas floating in a canal, water included. The fourth floor blooms pink with Sakura cherry blossoms, and features a herd of Hello Kitties and some high-tech Japanese toilets with warmed seats that wash your privates, the behind and the before, at the touch of a button, while playing music. One floor up, the American floor boasts the Golden Gate Bridge and a profusion of fast-food venues from Subway to KFC. All in all, Terminal 21 is a fun place to explore. One could spend hours studying its clever details, from the fluffy fake bird in a Parisian cage to the Japan Rail train station. But we weren't there to wander. We were there to find a safari jacket. And we did.

Believe it or not, Timberland had just the right thing. The perfect tan color, the correct pockets, the stiff fabric. Most surprisingly, it even fit. Except for my head (and the rest of me), I looked just like Mariska Hargitay. The giraffes would be delighted. Steve too. I bet he'd like a stylish safari companion looking like she dropped from Hollywood.

But I couldn't bring myself to buy it. In a country where most families live on less than 300 baht/day (about $8), a delicious lunch costs only a dollar or two, and the bus to the airport costs less than five dollars, how can I justify paying almost 400 dollars for a jacket I'll likely never wear again? No can do.

I bought a cheap khaki fleece and went home. Sorry, giraffes.

CHAPTER 11
ON THE ROAD AGAIN

THE DAYS after that crawled like snails through molasses. The Permethrin arrived on Saturday, all $180 of it — $20 for the content, $160 for the shipping. Ridiculous, I know, but that was the best I could do, and I took a deep sigh of relief as Steve sprayed his clothes. We packed the whole Sunday and Monday, lighter and lighter each time, until we trimmed it down to one medium roll on, one small duffle, and two half-empty backpacks, plus the camera bag and the computer bag with our iPads and my laptop.

When the time came to empty the fridge, take out the garbage, and look around for the last time, the reality of the trip stared me in the face and I started having second thoughts. Like so many times before, I looked in the mirror, spat the toothpaste, and asked myself: What on earth was I thinking? That's a question I ask myself often, but I rarely find an answer. Does that ever happen to you?

We headed out as the sun was going down, half-hoping we'd miss the plane. The anxiety was taking over, and we were worried. Not about getting eaten by hungry predators — I bet they can find tastier things than a couple of old chewy Americans. Not even about getting hijacked for ransom or getting bitten by venomous critters, even though I read that the black mamba, Kenya's deadliest snake, is aggressive when cornered and can reach up to twelve MPH to my three, even though I have two feet and he has none.

We worried about much more mundane things that tend to grow more important as you age. With so much time on the road and no rest stops to speak of, will we find toilets when we need them? What if we get sick? We won't drink unbottled water or eat leafy salads or unpeeled fruit, though I won't go so far as to wash my teeth with bottled water. But what if we get in trouble? How will we find medical care? How will we shower? And how will we stay in touch? Will we find any internet? Will Air Kenya prove to be a bad idea? How about that cheap bus?

"What if we just stayed here?" I asked Steve. "Nobody needs to know. We could download a few safari pictures off the internet, photo-shop us in, and send them to Tim."

He laughed, but he appeared thoughtful.

"We have travel insurance," he said. "We'd just have to go see a doctor for something to get an excuse." And, at our age, there's no shortage of things to see a doctor for. Easy-peasy.

But, being who we are, we pushed through. We grabbed our bags, locked the door, and headed down in an elevator full of people who didn't appear to care much for our luggage, meager as it was. All but an old American who wanted to know where we were from.

That's the thing about Americans. That's the first question that always pops up whenever Americans meet. I bet that's the first thing they'd talk about if they met on a deserted island after a boat wreck. I can just see it:

An exhausted, thirsty man crawls out of the surf, breathing hard and holding on to his only garment: A baseball cap with his favorite football team's logo.

The starving wild man sitting on the beach perks up. He shelters his eyes from the sun, struggling to make up the faded letters.

"Hey! Where are you from?"

"Oshkosh, Wisconsin. How about you?"

"Hey! A Packers fan! I'm from Tulsa!"

"Really? Who'd have thought? My neighbor's hairdresser's cousin's stepson went to Tulsa for college!"

"A small world, isn't it?" The man nods, licking his parched lips.

I seldom noticed anything like that in other people. Romanians commiserate over prices and bond over their intimate health issues; English people discuss the weather, and Italians talk about nothing but food. The only ones who even come close are the Thai. They'll stop you whilst crossing the street to ask where you are from and how old you are, like it's any of their business. But I digress.

The first Baht Bus we tried to stop gave us a wide berth. So did the second, then a third. They didn't like our bags, I bet. I started feeling hopeful that we'd miss the plane through no fault of our own, when the fourth bus stopped, sealing our fate.

We get to the airport bus with time to spare, and I grab the best seats in the house while Steve deals with the luggage. Half an hour later, we're zooming north on the highway with three dozen of our new close friends. The seats are roomy, the air is conditioned, and it's too late to turn around. Two hours later, in the check-in line, I stare in wonder at the many normal-ish looking people pushing mountains of bags taller than them. How on earth do they deal with it? And why?

"I don't want to ever hear you say we don't travel light," I tell Steve, who's been complaining bitterly about my shoes: One pair of boots, one of sandals, and crocs to wear in the tent.

He ignores me to cut in line ahead of a young couple who

can't see the check-in booth because of their luggage. Our two bags together are 19 kg (we're allowed 20 kg each) and I start reminiscing about all the things I could have packed. A few real books, and that piece of cheddar cheese I threw away, and...

Too late. The bags slide away, and, boarding passes in hand, we get swallowed by the unwieldy monster that is Bangkok's Suvarnabhumi Airport. Suvarnabhumi is to airports what blue wildebeests are to antelopes: massive, clumsy, and totally devoid of logic. But speaking about flying, there's Steve's take on Kenya Airways.

Kenya Airways

When we looked for the most convenient way to get from our Thai winter home to Kenya, we discovered that Kenya Airways operates a nonstop between Bangkok and Nairobi about three days a week, so we adjusted our safari dates accordingly and booked round-trip tickets for January.

The flight to Nairobi was delayed on takeoff by about two hours. One of those hours we spent standing in a bus on the apron after a gate issue. Accordingly, our safari started late from Nairobi. Fortunately, our driver/guide Francis was waiting and took over from the airport.

It's a nine-hour overnight flight each way. We've invested in business class flights since becoming senior citizens. The Kenya Air flight from Bangkok was an aging Boeing 787 with open lie-flat seats. The seats are arranged in a 2-2-2 configuration. Each seat in the middle has an aisle, but the passengers in the window seats have to climb over their neighbor to get out. That makes accessing the bathroom difficult and inconvenient in the night's darkness.

The seats have a lot of leg room in the seated position, but not quite enough room to lie flat if you're over six feet tall. The cubby hole next to the bed houses the TV remote and power plugs. It is sloped slightly toward the bed so it will deposit anything you place there into the bed mechanism for crushing. It got my phone on the way down and their TV remote on the return trip.

They offered the customary choice of drinks soon after boarding, but when we chose water, the attendant told us to look in the side pocket.

There are about thirty seats arranged in two cabins, with two toilets between the cabins and one more forward in the galley. But the cabin staff kept the forward toilet locked for their own use the entire flight, directing people to the remaining crowded two.

The return flight took off from Nairobi at midnight and, because of the four-hour time difference, landed in Bangkok at one p.m. The staff served a light meal after takeoff when everyone wanted to sleep, then lunch an hour before landing, when everyone was waking up and could have used breakfast, starting with some coffee. When asked, they explained they based their meals on the destination time zone.

We'll avoid Kenya Airways in the future.

CHAPTER 12
TO-DO LIST

AS WE FINALLY BOARD OUR flight two hours late, I start my to-do list, because no matter how exhausted we'll be, there are a few things we have to do after arriving in Nairobi.

1. Get through passports and customs. Steve got us Kenyan eVisas, so we shouldn't have to queue for that. With a bit of luck, they won't care about the instant coffee I brought with us. I go nowhere without instant coffee, since without a big jolt of caffeine, I can't make it to wherever it is they serve coffee. So that should be fine, but what they do seem to care about are plastic bags. My research indicates that bringing plastic bags to Kenya — any plastic bags — is only slightly worse than smuggling heroin in, or elephant tusks out. If you're lucky, you pay a hefty fine. If you're not, you go to jail. And spending time in a Kenyan jail is more of an adventure than I'm ready for.

While I applaud their dedication to saving the environment, I don't know how to manage without zipper bags. Much to my regret, I unpacked my shoes from the plastic bags I had them in and did the same with my clothes. I usually compress them in zipper bags to take less space and make them easier to sort out. But toothpaste? Shampoo? DEET? All likely to spit out their contents with the pressure change and mess up everything else in the bag? I put them all together in a zipper bag, praying they won't shoot me, or whatever their punishment is for that particular criminal offense. Hopefully, given my age, I'll get away with a short jail term.

2. Acquire Kenyan shillings. I tried everything, even Facebook, but I couldn't find them in Thailand. I did, however, entertain the IQ-challenged keyboard warriors who sent me to Kenya to find them. Getting a bit of cash to buy water, snacks, and other essentials would be handy, even though difficult at 6 a.m. Still, our friend George assured us there would be no problem, since the Nairobi airport functions 24/7. We shall see.

3. Get a SIM card for the phone. Some of our lodgings are supposed to have Wi-Fi in the common areas, but we're both internet dependent — Steve for the news, and me for everything else. And we need to keep in touch with our son and Guinness.

4. It would be wise to grab a bite before getting in the car, since we're both prone to motion sickness, and an empty stomach spells disaster. We're supposed to meet our driver/guide Francis and head straight to Samburu National Park, six hours away, on what, by all accounts, are terrible roads.

5. Finally, we'll meet Francis and go. From everything I've read, our driver/guide/minder will be our constant companion for the coming two weeks. He'll keep us safe, take us to the best viewing places, tell us what we're looking at, and help us out if we get in trouble. A driver/mother/teacher/guide combo that could make or break our trip, they say, so I really hope we get along. You know how you sometimes dislike people at first sight? Whether it's how they look, how they act, or the fact they can't stop talking — whatever gets on your nerves — I hope Francis is not one of those. And I really hope that between his English and our American we can communicate.

I'm pondering all this while Steve complains about the flight, the service, and life in general. I take a deep breath and pat his hand.

"Let's try to be positive instead of letting ourselves get consumed by everything that's not as expected and worry about everything that needs doing. This is our first day in Kenya. Just think: by tonight, all of this will be over, and we'll be in our lodge in the savannah. We'll even have had our first game drive and maybe even see some animals. Let's try to be positive, instead of worrying about plastic bags, jail, and SIM cards."

Steve cuts his eyes to me.

"I wouldn't worry about the SIM card either. Even if we manage to get one, it won't work for more than 15 minutes."

"Why?" I ask. "You think data is that expensive?"

Steve shakes his head.

"The thing will stop working as soon as we leave Nairobi. I bet there's no phone coverage anywhere else."

"Now that's thinking positive," I agree.

CHAPTER 13
THE FIRST DAY

We made it.

As I sit up in bed, wrapped in blankets to my chin and dressed in Steve's new t-shirt bought from 7-11 (that's the only thing I could find in the dark in our ransacked luggage) plus the khaki fleece I scrimped on, I have no regrets. I wouldn't be any warmer, and I'd look silly in that expensive safari jacket, even though it's too dark to see myself. It's 3 a.m. in Samburu as I write this, and there's no power, just like every night from midnight to five plus a few odd hours through the day. Around our palatial tent, the savanna hums with life like a simmering pot as the voices of countless wild creatures going about their lives blend into a soothing background sound. Every once in a while, a self-impressed cricket chirps louder than the rest, someone roars, or a branch cracks, making me wonder who's stalking who out there. But in here, I'm snug and content, awaiting an exciting DAY 2. In the meantime, let me tell you about DAY 1.

We were two hours late landing in Nairobi. We rushed out, hoping that Francis hadn't started without us. On the way out, we found a money exchange and changed $300 from Steve's money belt (152 shillings to a dollar) and then went through passport control, where the unsmiling, bored officers treated us like we were a nuisance. We collected our luggage and went through customs and luggage X-ray, where no one gave a damn about my plastic bag. I still wonder why they x-rayed our bags as we left. To see if we'd stolen any airplane parts? Or if our suitcases got pneumonia in the luggage compartment? Either way, we were out before I could say Merry Christmas in Swahili — I still can't — and found ourselves in a large arrival hall. The place was chock-full of helpful people elbowing each other to offer us a ride, but it sported none of the usual facilities, like shops, restrooms, restaurants, and car rentals. And no Francis.

Oops.

We dragged out our luggage, refusing the many offers of help and avoiding the countless hands that tried to grab it, hoping it was the right thing to do. We'll just come back if Francis is gone and we need a ride to a hotel, I thought.

Outside, straight across from the exit, three shacks advertised the very best SIM cards and roaming programs in Kenya. We gawked at them, wondering which was the best of the best, when Steve spotted Francis. At least we hoped so, since he held a sheet of paper with my name.

We shook hands, and I dispatched him with Steve to get a SIM card while I staunchly defended our luggage against the helpful hands trying to grab it to take it away.

The boys returned before I lost the fight, and we got moving. We started with a nice long march to our safari vehicle. We found it twenty minutes later, just as I'd started to wonder if it was waiting for us in Samburu. I expected a small run-down SUV, but our vehicle was nothing like that. Standing taller than Steve, with enough room to sit seven, our safari vehicle looked more like a World War II tank than a car, outside and in. That's why I named it Tank. Heavy metal doors almost impossible to open sealed the rear, holding a shovel, two spare tires, and various other equipment. The front had a tall antenna thicker than my arm and a high snorkel for air intake, so the engine wouldn't get flooded when crossing riverbeds. And if the outside looked sturdy, the inside must have seen more action than Steve and I put together and was built to last rather than dazzle. The seats were more comfortable than luxurious, and the boxy thing between the back seats that I hoped was a camp toilet turned out to be a fridge. But let's hear our engineer's take on the vehicle:

The safari vehicles are all heavy-duty Toyota Land Cruiser pickup trucks with a custom "safari" body from the cab back. They come in either a two-row, five-passenger version like ours, or, more commonly, a three-row, seven-passenger "extended" model for larger groups.

There are no Land Rovers on safari despite Kenya's British heritage. When asked why, Francis explained that Land Rovers are too expensive and less reliable. I still remember my father telling me about supplying Land Rovers as part of an oil pipeline project in Libya. Part way through the contract, the Libyans forced him to take back all the expensive Land Rovers and replace them with more reliable Toyota Land Cruisers.

All safari Land Cruisers in the parks had heavy off-road tires with two spares mounted on the rear. Most had pop-open roofs like ours, but a few had roll-up canvas side curtains. In the pop-top versions, the passengers can stand up to view or photograph over the vehicle roof. In the others, they remain seated and roll up the curtains.

The truck suspensions are so stiff they practically launch you out of the vehicle when negotiating the deeply rutted trails. The vehicle has a diesel engine and a five-speed manual trans-

mission. The diesel is great for the bush, but has a lot of trouble on the highways between parks and getting up the hills.

As I had recommended, Steve claimed the front seat, which was loaded with Francis's stuff. I had suggested that sitting there would allow him to see better and make him less prone to motion sickness. He'd also get a chance to speak to Francis, so I'd have some peace in the back, but I didn't mention that. More importantly, I managed to dissuade him from trying to drive — for now, at least.

A bit surprised but gracious, Francis made room. We loaded our luggage and got on our way.

The six-hour drive from the airport to Samburu, our first day's destination, was more exciting than restful. The roads were narrow and busy but not bad, except for the many detours around work areas. No matter where you looked, there was an endless stream of new construction, since Kenya is a young country and it's growing fast. The Kenyans' life expectancy is sixty-seven, but the median age is only nineteen, and new families need a place to live. Construction materials abound, and so do markets of every kind, from the one-man fruit stands selling pineapples and mangoes to whole-town affairs offering everything from corn, rice, and tomatoes to skinny cows, clucking chickens, and bleating goats.

Francis kindly answered my endless stream of questions. His English was excellent, even though our conflicting accents would occasionally get in the way.

"What are those?" I asked, pointing to a long display of large fabrics hanging on a fence across the street. Some were colorful, some plain, some printed. Here and there, big coils of rope hung in between.

"Carnivals," Francis said.

"Carnivals?" I asked in astonishment. They didn't look that colorful. And I saw no animals and no clowns.

"Carnivals," he confirmed, and stopped to talk to the woman in charge.

How odd, I thought. Maybe the carnival is behind the fence?

"It's 7500 each, depending on the size," Francis confirmed after speaking to the woman, then pulled back into the traffic.

"For a carnival?" I was befuddled. How do you buy a carnival? What would you do with it? And what sort of carnival is only 60 bucks?

Francis nodded, leaving me to my confusion.

Steve choked with laughter.

"It's canvas," he chortled. "Not carnivals. Canvas."

I tried to kick him, but he was too far to reach.

A few similar incidents kept us entertained until we stopped to get gas and use the washrooms, as Francis calls them. We also purchased some snacks, but it turned out that the Snickers bar Francis bought was already opened. Good to know I should check next time, I told myself, and offered him some of the delicious potato chips with salt and vinegar I had purchased for seventy shillings — less than fifty cents. The chili ones were tasty too, but the chocolate-filled cookies not so much.

We continued north on long stretches of roads edged with tiny buildings looking like old tool sheds covered with corrugated metal. They sported bright colors and exciting labels like "Vision Milk Cafe," "Peacock and Pebbles Garden," and "God's Favor Hotel."

How can that be a hotel? I wondered, staring at the windowless shed with its door hanging open. But then "Primacare Hotel and Pork Center," caught my attention, and just as I started wondering what a pork center was, we saw the "Acacia Pork Center and Club." Kenyan pigs seemed to have a lively social life, with all their centers and clubs, unlike the many cows and sheep who just graze along the road.

Between them sat dozens of similar-looking financial and IT institutions, from "Netflix Cyber," and "White House Insurance," to "Galaxy Investment" that didn't look sky-high successful at investing. Every fifth building seemed to be some sort of Christian establishment, whether Adventist, Orthodox, Catholic, or Protestant. Whether made of bricks, mud, or corrugated metal, they all called for the faithful to gather and praise the Lord. The schools, especially the girls' schools, all had Christian names invoking the Virgin. Once in a while, a mosque broke the monotony, especially further north towards Somalia. I couldn't help but notice that Kenyans are very faithful people.

We drove and drove until our bums got sore and our backs started aching. Francis proved to be a cautious driver, keenly aware of the many things waiting to throw themselves under Tank's wheels, from dogs, goats, and kids to a whole pack of baboons in a terrible hurry. He gave them all a wide berth. We went on and on, passing rows of parked camels grazing the meager dusty grass along the road, thousands of athletic cows with sinewy muscles and long, sharp horns but not one ounce of fat that chewed their cud, and herds of sheep and goats with playful kids watched by skinny young men with long sticks. It was fascinating, but we were running late for lunch, and we were starving.

As soon as he left the main road to turn onto the unpaved road to our camp, Francis pushed the pedal to the metal. Roaring, cracking, and screeching, Tank leaped from rock to rock, leaning dangerously right and left before righting itself on the bottom of some pothole and starting over. The engine vroomed, dust darkened the sky, and my joints loosened as Francis tackled that track that didn't deserve to be called a road at full speed.

I had a blast. I held on to my chair with both hands so I wouldn't fly out through the ceiling, and laughed like a hyena, with my teeth clenched to avoid biting my tongue. Steve, who had taken my seat in the back, not so much. His eyes had glazed, and his face turned green from motion sickness. But we had no time to stop. The people at the lodge waited with our lunch, and we were already late. We drove furiously past a few Grant's gazelles, a well-fed zebra, some antelopes, and two ostriches shaking their tail feathers. We stopped for a moment to take a picture of a lonely elephant, then crossed a shallow river and chased away a monitor lizard, before darting through the Ashnil Samburu Lodge's gates, our home for the next two nights. Twenty minutes later, well shaken and thoroughly stirred, we stumbled to the ground amid half a dozen people waiting for us.

"Welcome to Samburu."

CHAPTER 14
THE FIRST GAME DRIVE

ALL THAT WAS YESTERDAY. Now I'm still in bed, writing. It's almost five, but there's no sign of the power coming back. But thankfully, despite Steve's ominous premonitions, the SIM card still works. We still have a cell signal, even though we're hundreds of miles from Nairobi and many kilometers from the grid. Hard to believe, but Steve's not always right.

The Ashnil Samburu lodge is a compound of sturdy abodes they call tents, surrounded by an electric fence. The central area has a restaurant, a gift shop, and a tiny pool, besides an amazing number of people whose only goal in life seems to be to make you comfortable.

Our lunch was waiting, even though the schedule said that the restaurant should have been closed for an hour. The menu offered us choices of salads, soups, entrees, and desserts, and the beverage list did not disappoint. The Greek salad was tasty, Steve's fish with lemon delicious, and my steak with pepper was not too chewy. The fruit was nice too, but the cheese plate not so much. An interesting point: Though this lodge is an all-included resort, you pay for drinks. Not only the alcohol, but also the water. A small bottle of water will set you back 2–3 dollars, a beer 4–5, and a cocktail around 6.

After lunch, we finally made it to our "tent," which is a large bedroom with a comfortable four-poster king bed with mosquito nets, a desk, a fan, and a well-equipped ensuite bathroom. The water gets heated with firewood, and it's available from 5 to 9 in the morning and evening. There's no AC, but the screens allow for the free flow of fresh air and occasional helicopter-sized insects with a rambunctious personality and a propensity for the shower. The screen doors are zipped and attached with carabiners to prevent the ubiquitous Vervet monkeys from entering to steal and trash everything inside, as they apparently love to do. These crafty cat-sized critters are everywhere — grooming each other on the lawn, perched up in the trees, chasing each other across the roofs. Round-eyed babies no bigger than a kitten cling to their mom's bellies and coil their tail around hers so it doesn't drag on the ground, while males show off their amazing aqua-blue testicles to charm the ladies. They love raiding the tables at the restaurant, so much so that there's a full-time guard with a slingshot keeping them out. Mostly.

After 24 hours on the road, that bed looked awfully inviting. We wished we could linger for a bit, but it was time to meet Francis for our first game drive. So we ransacked our luggage, looking for fresh clothes, but, seeing there was no hot water to shower, we gave up and wore the same clothes we'd left home with. I didn't think the wildlife would care.

Five minutes early, Francis was waiting. He'd popped up Tank's roof, allowing us to stand in the back and take pictures unencumbered.

That drive was nothing like the mad dash that had brought us to the lodge an hour earlier, when we seemed ready to run over half of Kenya's wildlife. But now, forewarned maybe, the animals stuck to their covers. A bunch of Grant's gazelles grazed in the distance — this Grant seemed to have a lot of gazelles. They are beautiful, strong animals, standing 3 feet to the shoulder, with a tan-orange coat and a white behind, lyre-shaped ringed horns and smoldering dark eyes. And they are, fortunately, not endangered.

We passed by a few chatty birds, and we stopped at a shallow river crossing to wonder at a dead crocodile stuck at the edge. The thing was not massive — only about 6 feet long — lying with his white belly up, swollen, and missing his lower jaw. And it smelled like it had been there for a while.

"What kills crocodiles?" I asked Francis.

He shrugged.

"I don't know. Can't think of anything, because of their thick skin. In fact, I don't think I've seen a dead crocodile before."

Just our luck. This guy watches animals for a living, and he's never seen this. And we just landed from the other side of the world and there we are, knee-deep in mystery and breathing its aroma to boot. A mystery needing solving? We're ready.

"Do crocodiles kill each other?" I asked.

Francis shook his head.

"Rarely."

"So you think he died from natural causes? Like a heart attack or such?"

"Maybe."

"But then, where's the missing jaw? A heart attack wouldn't make it lose its jaw, would it?"

Francis shrugged. The medical history of crocodiles was obviously not high on his list of priorities.

"Unless he died for some reason or other, and then someone ate it. Who eats crocodiles?"

Francis must have tired of my questions, or maybe of the

smell, because he drove forward, leaving the stinky carcass behind.

"Look, elephants," he said, with the same voice I used to distract my toddler son when he got fixated on a toy I didn't want to buy.

But he was right. An elephant, floppy ears, tusks, and all, headed towards us, munching on a thorny branch that looked like it would hurt to touch. We forgot all about the crocodile and started snapping pictures, when another elephant followed, this one a baby.

Holding our breaths with excitement, we stumbled all over each other to take pictures as they got closer and closer. Mrs. Elephant snorted and waved her trunk at us.

"Move on, humans. Nothing to see here. Move along now," she seemed to say.

Regretfully, Francis inched Tank further to clear her way. But before we'd moved 30 feet, another elephant blocked the path.

This one glanced at us sideways, lowered her trunk, and took a big snort of dust that she proceeded to spray over her back.

"She's taking a bath," Francis said.

No shampoo, no washcloth, no nothing.

"Well, if she thinks she'll get any cleaner." I shrugged.

She stepped across the road, and a baby elephant followed, this one even smaller than the first, flopping his dumbo-like ears and flicking his tail. He was having a grand old time with the dust, and we started taking pictures again, but the elephants behind us got annoyed.

"Move along, humans, I said." Mrs. Elephant pointed her tusks at our spare tire.

We would have been glad to oblige, but the mother and baby ahead of us lingered in the dust, soon followed by another mother and her baby, then another, even larger, matron, who kept her small shrewd eyes glued to us. Where could we go? Elephants behind, elephants ahead, and bushes everywhere else. With elephants dusting themselves all around us, I felt like a cat trapped at a kids' pool party. Unwilling, but stuck.

We waited, hoping they'd move on. They did, but not before another, even larger elephant, stepped out of the bushes.

"That's the bull," Francis whispered in awe.

He was massive. And impressive. But he wasn't the boss of this herd.

The matriarch, a large wrinkled female carrying her age with the graceful nonchalance of Willy Nelson, moved away from the path and the other ones followed. First the mothers with their babies, then the bull, bringing up the rear. That was awesome.

After a few more birds and antelopes, we finally headed back for dinner and a much-needed rest.

"See you at 7," Francis said.

That was yesterday. Now it's 6 a.m.

CHAPTER 15
DAY 2 — BUFFALO SPRINGS

Soon after 5 a.m., just as I started losing hope, the generator finally roared to life, and the power came back, bringing with it enough light to find our way to the bathroom, charging our phones and computer, and turning on the kettle for coffee. But not before I'd started wondering what would happen if someone had a serious emergency during those dark hours of midnight to five. What if someone had a stroke, a heart attack, or a nasty fall? Most cardiovascular events tend to happen in the early morning, and falls are way more likely in the dark. So what if we got in trouble? There's no phone, and the walk to the reception — should anyone be available there — is a long way through the park in the dark. Between the Vervet monkeys eyeing your camera, the elephants scratching their backs by the fence, and the chameleons running between your feet, that trip is an adventure even at noon. At night, if badness happens, you're pretty much on your own.

But so are you if you climb Kilimanjaro, sail across the ocean, or live off the grid. It's a risk you assume if you decide it's worth it. If we wanted a low-risk vacation, we should have gone to an all-inclusive resort.

The sun rose over the savanna for another exciting day. At seven sharp we climbed into Tank with our camera, the binoculars, and my iPhone, and off we went.

We headed towards Buffalo Springs, a waterhole made by the Germans when they bombed Kenya in World War II. After missing whatever military objective they had sought, they dropped their bombs in the savanna, creating a spa for the buffaloes to congregate at.

The round concrete hole filled with milky-blue water was deserted at first, but before long, two ostriches came by. The darker male first, shaking his fluffy tail feathers, followed by the lighter, drabber female. Which brings me to a discovery: In the animal world, with few exceptions, the male is the looker. He spiffs himself up in all ways to conquer the female's heart — and her other body parts — and goes to a lot of trouble to wow her, even it's only for a one-night stand. It's the same for the peacocks, the lions, the ducks, and just about every gazelle and antelope we met. The males are bigger, brighter, and more glamorous, whether they choose to dazzle their mates with their sexy dark mane, glamorous tail, elegant horns, or bright blue testicles. No effort is too much, since the male's only hope of reproducing is to conquer a female that will carry his seed.

Females, however, are choosy. No matter how small and drab, they look for the strongest, best-looking, and craftiest male they can mate with to endow their progeny with the best DNA and give them the best chance to survive. That's why, in the animal kingdom, from lions and chimpanzees to impalas and zebras, a few males have large harems while many others will be incels, living a life of forced celibacy with little chance to reproduce.

We were still watching the long-legged ostriches dance their can-can when a silhouette on the horizon caught our attention.

It had a long, sloped neck, a tiny head, and long spindly legs at odd angles.

"A giraffe," Francis said, and stepped on the accelerator, kicking back a cloud of dust. He rushed not to chase her — he couldn't catch her even if she stayed on the road, because giraffes can sprint up to 35 mph , and Tank can't get near that on these trails — but to intercept her. Sure enough, after a few unexpected turns when we thought we'd lost her, we were there, waiting, when the giraffe stopped to look left and right before crossing the road, like all pedestrians should. She stopped to let us pass, but we politely declined and waited for her to determine that we weren't a menace. It took a minute, but she eventually ambled across the road towards wherever giraffes have their morning coffee.

She balanced her long, heavy neck and swung her gangly legs as if she had to count to see whose turn came next. She was a reticulated giraffe, so her warm cinnamon-colored skin looked covered in a white see-through net, giving her a pattern as unique as our fingerprints. Her ossicles, the little hornlike projections decorating her head, were shorter than her white-backed mobile ears that never stopped moving, making her look like she had a tiny windmill on her head.

I have a soft spot for giraffes, so that got me really excited. Even more so when I spotted a group of them at the other end of the savanna, minutes later.

Getting anywhere near them in this massive territory with few tracks and plenty of obstacles, like thorny bushes, massive umbrella-like acacia trees, and dry riverbeds seemed unlikely, but Francis did it again. Minutes later, we were waiting for the five of them to cross. But they didn't.

They stopped to stare at us a hundred feet away. They glanced at each other, then back at us. They twitched their noses, sniffed our way, and whipped their long, tasseled tails, looking worried.

The smallest one, which must have been just a baby, seemed particularly vexed. He stopped behind the largest giraffe and stared at her as if asking her what to do.

"Stay here," Big Mama must have said, because he didn't move as she stepped closer to investigate our intentions. Two others followed, looking, listening, and sniffing us as we stood frozen, watching their silent conversation.

The fourth one didn't. Acting like nothing worried him in the least, he turned his back on the encounter to munch on a spiny acacia bush.

Big Mama took one last look at us and determined we were either dead or too lazy to move, so she turned to her young.

"Common, baby. Let's get going. We don't have all day."

We heard nothing, but he did. He shook his head, swished his tail, and galloped to join the pack. Tall, dignified, and ungainly, like a group of arthritic English aristocrats leaving their club after one drink too many, they crossed the road just feet ahead of us, ambling towards greener pastures.

The fourth one stayed behind and kept munching on his bush.

The others turned to look at him.

"Hey, Braxton. Are you coming or what?"

Braxton ignored them.

Big Mama shook her head and lengthened her stride. I could almost hear her.

"Today's teenagers…"

They'd covered some distance when young Braxton noticed they were gone. With an agility I didn't think giraffes could muster, he curled up his tail and sped to a gallop, moving his hind legs around the front legs, and bobbing his small head balanced on the long neck to keep his balance. Before long, he closed the distance to the others, leaving behind a cloud of dust.

If you want to learn a little bit about giraffes, their fascinating anatomy, physiology, and behavior, read the next chapter: On Giraffes. If not, skip it and move on.

CHAPTER 16
ON GIRAFFES

At 20 feet tall and 3,000 hefty pounds, the giraffe is the tallest animal and the largest ruminant on Earth. Her heart alone weighs 25 pounds and is 2 feet long, about as big as a French Bulldog, attitude included. Compared to that, an average human heart weighs less than a pound.

Giraffes are thought to have evolved from an ancestor called Sivatherium, which resembled a giant antelope, before going through the evolutionary adaptations we see today.

The three existent giraffe subspecies are distinguished by their distinctive coats that earned them the name of camelopard. The coat pattern serves as camouflage, helping them blend into the dappled light of savannas and woodlands. Every pattern is as unique as our fingerprints, allowing researchers to tell them apart, but they recognize each other by smell.

The giraffe's 18-inch-long tongue is black, to protect it from sunburn, and so nimble that it can peel the fresh tiny leaves off the thorny acacia branches protected by two-inch-long spines that are their favorite food. They also eat fruits, flowers, and whatever greens they can find.

Thanks to their four stomachs, giraffes spend a lot of time

on their favorite hobby, which is chewing the cud. The half-masticated leaves picked from the treetops slide down their long throats into the first stomach where they mix with the gastric juices to form a bolus that returns to the mouth whenever the giraffe is not busy eating, like when she's listening to the bush news or watching the kids. That's when she re-chews the bolus into a paste, then sends it down to the next stomach where her digestive system, which includes over 200 feet of intestine, extracts every last bit of nutrient before pooping it out. Unlike humans, giraffes have no gallbladder. That may be why they never indulge in French fries. They only eat greens, over 75 pounds a day, and then poop them out as small pellets.

The giraffe's most distinctive feature, their long neck, is also their most powerful weapon. While most animals fight with their teeth and claws, giraffes fight with their necks. To decide who gets the girl, male giraffes rub their necks and slap each other silly with their heads until one of them gets knocked out or quits. The ladies appreciate the attention, but that doesn't necessarily mean they're available, i.e., in heat. The ossicones help with thermoregulation, acting like radiators to dissipate heat, and signal dominance during necking fights.

To gauge a female's availability, the male nudges her behind until she pees, then tastes her urine with the fierce concentration of a passionate enologist assessing a new vintage. But while the enologist checks the wine's acidity, tannins, and aromas, the giraffe looks for the hormones indicating that the lady is in estrus before asking her out.

A courting male will lick a female's tail, lay his head on her neck, or nudge her with his ossicones. If she's interested, romance often ensues, but it's usually short-lived.

Giraffes' gestation lasts 400–460 days (that's about 15 months, an awful long time if you ask me) resulting in a single calf taller than a grown human who can stand just a few minutes after birth and can run in a few hours. Still, for the first few weeks, the calf is extremely vulnerable, so it stays hidden.

Adult giraffes can live up to forty years. Because of their size and powerful kicks, they have no natural predators other than lions. Their calves, however, are hunted by leopards, spotted hyenas, and wild dogs, so less than a third of newborns reach adulthood.

Male giraffes are deadbeat dads more interested in having sex than having kids. Once the courtship is over, the mothers are on their own. That's why they organize in savanna-type PTOs where the moms take turns chaperoning the young and going out for dinner. They will even suckle each other's babies.

As for humans, drinking is a risky business for giraffes. First, because predators love to hide and stalk prey around watering holes. Second, because of their height. Lifting their heads from water level to their full height should normally drain all the blood from their brain and starve it of oxygen. A human would pass out, but giraffes don't, thanks to the rete mirabile, a complex network of blood vessels that acts like a sponge, filling with blood when the giraffe lowers her head, then draining slowly as she lifts it, helping keep the brain oxygenated. Giraffes are binge drinkers. They don't need to drink daily, but they need their fill every three days.

Giraffes sleep only four to five hours a day in the wild, often in short bursts, to avoid predation. They usually sleep standing up, though deep sleep may involve lying down and curling their necks backward.

Giraffes are often infested with ticks, especially around their genitals where the skin is thinner. That's why they rely on the red and yellow-billed oxpecker hygienists. Oxpeckers, as the name indicates, are birds that make a living by relieving giraffes, buffaloes, and hippos of their parasite burden. They also alert them of incoming dangers. In exchange, giraffes provide them with transportation and a scrumptious all-the-ticks-you-can-eat buffet.

Giraffes move the legs on the same side of the body to walk but move their legs in a clockwise fashion when they gallop, and curl up their tail for balance. They can sprint up to 35 mph, but not for long, because giraffes aren't into aerobics. Their lungs are small relative to their size, and their extra-long neck makes them breathe as if they're inhaling through a 10-foot-long snorkel.

Giraffes are silent most of the time because their vocal cords are not well-suited for vocalizing over their long necks, but they can snort, sneeze, cough, snore, hiss, burst, moan, grunt, and growl to communicate their feelings, just like teenagers asked to do chores or husbands harassed while watching TV. Their body language is also familiar: dominant males will walk on stiff legs and jut their chin, while submissive individuals will lower their heads.

Giraffes are classified as vulnerable from a conservation perspective. They are protected in national parks, but losing their habitat and the poaching for their skin and bushmeat are ongoing threats.

CHAPTER 17
DAY 2 — ELEPHANTS

DAY 2 MUST HAVE BEEN the day of the teenagers.

Soon after the giraffes disappeared, we happened upon a herd of elephants — a few mothers with their young of all ages, from babies to a teenager with longish tusks and an attitude to match. We stopped at a respectful distance to let them pass, but the young bull was curious. His mother tried to prompt him back, but no. He came closer. Much closer.

Francis pulled Tank back a tad.

The youth stepped forward.

His mother stomped her feet and headed back to the rest of the herd, looking back for him to follow, but he was on a mission. He came even closer.

The other elephants gathered across the road in the shade of the canopy and got their heads together, trying to figure out what to do. They flicked their tails, flapped their ears, and snorted clouds of dust, stomping their heavy feet to call his attention, but the youth couldn't care less. He only had eyes for Tank. He fanned his ears and douched himself with sand, while keeping his eyes on us, then started picking spiny branches from an acacia tree. Those poor acacias, they have it hard. The giraffes, with their mobile lips and long, skilled tongues, pick up the tiny leaves from between the thorns and leave the branches intact, but the elephants pull down whole branches, and sometimes they'll uproot entire trees. Quite rude, really, if you think that everyone in the savanna depends on those trees for survival.

There are over eight hundred different species of acacia in Africa. Thanks to their resilience and drought resistance, they provide food, shade, and shelter for people and animals, from elephants to ants. Native healers use their bark and leaves to relieve diarrhea and cure skin infections, and their gum serves as thickener in the food industry.

But our unruly teenage elephant couldn't care less about any of that. His eyes glued to Tank, he chewed thoughtfully on that spiny branch like it wasn't covered in two-inch thorns.

We waited. The pack of elephants snorted in the back.

After a few minutes of deep thinking, Junior threw his snack to the ground and stomped on it, then moved forward to charge us. When he got so close to the car that I worried his tusks would break the windshield, he flapped his ears and rose his trunk in a challenge.

But Francis had had it. Instead of backing up, like he had done every other time, he stepped on the acceleration, revved the engine, and inched Tank forward.

Taken aback by this unexpected development, the youth took a step back.

Francis inched forward again.

Thirty feet away, under the canopy, the grown-ups got worried. His mother snorted, flapped her ears, and stepped towards us, lifting her trunk to the sky. "Don't touch my baby," she said, and the message was just as clear as if she'd said it in English. "He may be an idiot, but he's mine."

But Junior had had enough. This ugly green thing, whatever

it was, behaved poorly. It stunk, it made horrific roaring noises, and it failed to give way. He wisely decided that he wanted nothing to do with us, so he gave us the stink eye, then turned around and joined the rest of the herd on the double.

Still, that wasn't the end of teenage antics for the day. The afternoon drive had more elephant meetings in store, one of them a schoolyard brawl.

We fell behind a large elephant herd grazing on top of a bushy ridge. There were at least twenty: a massive matriarch leading the pack, followed by a few mothers with young babies stuck to their side. Behind them trotted half a dozen youths, almost grown but not quite, by their size, tusks, and rotten attitude.

Snorting and flapping their ears, two of them head-butted each other right in front of the car. Seeing those sharp tusks cross so near their eyes made me shrink, but the encounter didn't take long. With more speed than grace, one of them pivoted, turned tail, and scampered into the bushes. Without missing a beat, the other one followed, trying to skewer the escapee's rear with his tusks.

I worried about what went on in the bushes, but seconds later, one of them burst back into a cloud of leaves and branches to challenge one of the peaceful onlookers.

A few ear flaps, a couple head butts, and another one turned tail, chased by the victor. I'd already lost track of who was who, since they weren't wearing their team colors, when someone came back from the bush to challenge another onlooker, and so on. Soon enough, there was only one left, and he turned towards us. His ears flapping, his trunk up in the air, he snorted and challenged us. I didn't know whether to worry about Tank or about the elephant's tusks when Francis revved the engine. Tank roared, and the bully took off into the bushes, expecting us to follow. But we didn't. We went on our way, watching the mothers and babies behave like nothing had happened.

Had they been human, an adult would have intervened to stop the silliness before someone got hurt, but not here. These childish brawls prepare them for adult life, when they'll have to duel for the ladies' affections or fight to protect their young, so they're part of their learning. But if so, what happens to the young who don't grow up in communities? Like leopards, cheetahs, and maybe even giraffes? How do they learn to fight? Instinct, maybe?

Samburu was our elephant paradise, besides a bunch of zebras and all sorts of antelopes that I can't keep straight. I can't tell a Grant gazelle from an impala or a Thompson's. They look the same to me, other than the oryx, whose long horns are hard to miss. And the tiny dik-dik, so small they could fit in my backpack, but so graceful and fully formed, from their miniature hooves to the tip of their cute little horns. Unlike other gazelles, the dik-dik are territorial and monogamous. They get their water from their food, so they don't need to drink. The female gives birth to a calf once to twice a year, and, even though they are so tiny that every predator is after them, from hyenas and wild dogs to lions and humans, their babies' survival rate is better than that of giraffes, and even lions, who lose more than half their cubs during the first year.

We also saw a lot of birds, from the tiny swallow weaver birds, no bigger than a walnut, who hang their grass-woven nests from the acacias, making them look like African Christmas trees, to the spectacular crowned cranes with their fluffy golden feathers, the white-headed fisher-eagles diving for fish from the treetops, and the silly-looking ostriches baring their shapely legs all the way to the business parts and shaking their fluffy derrieres like exotic dancers. A tortoise crossing the road ahead of us got stuck in the grasses, and for once, Francis allowed us to get out of the car to look at her. Her shell was chipped and cracked as if someone had stepped on her, but that didn't seem to bother her one bit. As soon as we untangled her from the tall grasses holding her captive, she got on her way in a hurry without looking back. Speak about ingratitude!

We saw lots of wildlife in our first park, but to me, Samburu belongs to the elephants. Protected from poachers, they can live as they like, in large, well-organized families where each knows their place and everyone looks after each other.

Before crossing a shallow river to head home, we had to wait for a herd of them to drink. One by one, they came to the river's edge to dip their trunks into the muddy water, then emptied it into their mouths again and again. It takes a lot of water to fill an elephant.

The large matriarch kept her eyes on us while gently flapping her ears to cool. A few babies stuck to their mothers like glue, pushing their hairy heads between the mothers' front legs, where the milk came from, but the females were busy drinking and getting their spa treatments. One of them dipped the delicate finger at the end of her trunk into the thick mud and stirred it with water into a slurry, then sucked it into her trunk and sprayed it over her back. She repeated the process until she was covered with mud, then sniffed a healthy serving of dust and blew it on top, coating herself in elephant-style sun protection, before leaving her spot to the next one. The babies got coated too, even the tiny tuskless twins who couldn't have been more than a month old and adorably hairy, the smallest elephants I'd ever seen. They all took their turn at the spa before heading into the bushes for dinner.

We left our last game drive in Samburu with a smile, even though we'd seen none of the big cats most tourists come to see.

"They're there, hiding," Francis had assured me the day

before, when I had tried to head into the grasses for you-know-what and he said no. "Just squat behind the car. We had more rain this season than we've had in years, so the grass is still tall. It would normally be burned by now, so we'd see the big cats stalking their prey, but not this year. That's why we have so many elephants."

A fiery sun bloodied the sky behind the acacia trees, and the warm wind caressing our faces smelled like crushed grasses, dust, and a hint of elephant dung, making up the scent of the savanna. It had been a good day.

If you want to learn more about the elephants' anatomy, social life, and behavior, read the next chapter, "On Elephants." Or skip it and move on.

CHAPTER 18
ON ELEPHANTS

AT 13 FEET tall and up to 16,000 pounds, elephants are the largest terrestrial animals. But even if they weren't, they'd still be easy to recognize by their long trunk, impressive tusks, and large fanning ears.

I must admit I'm in awe of their trunk. Other than a tail, which I would love to have because it would come in handy in so many instances of my daily living, from chasing flies to expressing my feelings, a trunk is the only extra body part I'd buy even if it wasn't on sale.

The elephant trunk is actually their upper lip fused with their nose, and it's boneless. Paired muscles, superficial and internal, connect to a bony prominence in the skull and work in concert to move the trunk, bending, twisting, stretching, and retracting it with extraordinary strength, impressive flexibility, and exquisite finesse. An elephant trunk can lift up to 800 pounds, pick leaves off treetops, dig in the mud, and suck two gallons of water to drink or shower with. It is also an excellent snorkel when crossing deep water, a sensitive nose better than those of many dogs, and a nimble finger.

The tusks are teeth. They are the second incisors in the upper jaw, replacing the milk teeth by one year of age and growing about 7 inches a year, up to 10 feet. When not used to fight for the ladies' attention, they dig for water, de-bark trees, and push around heavy stuff. Interestingly, elephant tusks are not symmetrical. One is usually more worn down, because, just like us, elephants are righties or lefties, and prefer to use their better side.

Their tough skin is one inch thick on the back and head, but much thinner around their mouth and inside the ears, and it requires mud baths for sunburn and insect protection. To maintain their temperature at 97°F, elephants flap their vascular ears to release excess heat.

Elephants' limbs are vertical to easier support their massive weight, which goes mostly on the front legs. Elephants can swim, but they don't run. They can quicken their stride to a march when they're in a hurry, but their legs are never simultaneously off the ground.

An average elephant brain weighs three times more than a human's but is proportionally smaller considering the weight difference.

Their 40-pound heart beats at only twenty-eight beats per minute compared to our seventy. To digest the 700 pounds of leaves, twigs, fruit, bark, grass, and roots they eat every day, their intestines reach 115 feet. But, unlike giraffes, elephants only absorb less than half of their nutrient intake, which is great news for the many freeloaders, from monkeys to ants, who feed on elephant dung.

Because of the tremendous impact they have on the environment, elephants are considered a keystone species. They uproot trees, transforming the savanna into grasslands, and dig for water, creating waterholes that sustain many other animals.

As they travel and poop, they disperse the seeds of the plants they eat and provide them with a substrate to grow, thus helping with carbon sequestration and indirectly helping with climate change.

Their impressive size makes adult elephants invulnerable, but the calves may get preyed upon, especially by lions. Females live in tightly knit matrilineal groups where the matriarch leads the group until death, then her eldest daughter takes over. Matriarchs remember the locations of water sources and safe routes, which are crucial for survival during droughts. During the dry season, when the food becomes scarce, a few families may aggregate to defend their range together.

Adult males live alone or in groups whose hierarchy depends on their age and size. Still, when male elephants go through musth, a testosterone-high phase that lasts for weeks, they become so aggressive that they win most fights, even against larger bulls.

Females only mate with one male, usually during rainfall. The bull assesses the cow's readiness by sampling her urine and jealously guards her from mating with other males, but the romance is short-lived, and mating takes less than a minute.

Gestation lasts up to two years, and most births happen during the wet season. The "tiny" newborn weighs 250 pounds and is 33 inches tall, and he's the center of everyone's attention. It takes him a month to start grabbing objects with his trunk, and three months to learn to forage and use his trunk to drink, but he continues to suckle until he's at least two. Females may become sexually mature by nine, but the males need a few more years. Adulthood starts around 18, and elephants can live until 70.

Elephants greet one another by touching their trunks. Touch is also essential for mother–calf communication: mothers always touch their calves with their trunks, or with their tails if the calf is behind them.

To deter attackers, elephants raise and shake their heads and trunks while spreading and snapping their ears. Their vocalizations — trumpeting, bellowing, roaring, growling, barking, snorting, and rumbling — carry over miles. For long-distance communication, elephants use infrasound, low-frequency sounds below human hearing, which can travel up to 10 miles, allowing them to coordinate movements or warn others of danger, or drum their feet to send seismic signals up to twenty miles.

Elephants are one of the few animals that show self-awareness by recognizing themselves in the mirror, like apes, dolphins, and most humans older than two. They use tools, like branches, to swat themselves from flies; they have an excellent memory and express empathy. When an elephant is in trouble, he will seek attention and get help from others, even if they are not related. Elephants grieve their dead. They will visit the bones of deceased elephants, touching them gently with their trunks, and will stay with a dying elephant to comfort it.

African elephants have some legal protection in all the countries they live in, but they are still an endangered species. Successful conservation efforts increased their numbers in some countries like Kenya, but in others, they continue to decline because of poaching and habitat loss.

Elephants are poached for their ivory, meat, and hide. To prevent further decline, some countries have banned ivory trade. Kenya destroyed all its ivory stocks. Zimbabwe, Botswana, Namibia, Zambia, and Malawi continue to trade ivory, but only from culled individuals or those dead of natural causes. Supposedly.

Another major threat to elephants is the destruction and fragmentation of their habitat. Without room to roam, hungry elephants destroy crops and villages, getting in conflict with humans and putting both elephants and humans at risk. One proposed solution is creating wildlife protection corridors, allowing elephant populations to connect. To protect crops, new solutions include electric fences, chili pepper products, and creating beehive barriers, since elephants who don't fear lions and leopards are afraid of bees. Go figure!

CHAPTER 19
MONEY MATTERS

AFTER A RICH BREAKFAST WITH EGGS, bacon, and sausage made to order, excellent Kenyan coffee, fruit, and an unimpressive spread of bread and pastries, we settled our accounts — about $30 spent on water and a couple drinks — left $50 in the tip box for the staff, and left the Ashnil Samburu Lodge heading southwest to Ol Pejeta

A word on tips in Kenya: They are always expected and never enough. Fodor's guide recommends $10–15 per person per day for the entire resort staff to divide, less for a family. We left a bit more than that, but I couldn't help but feel that everyone expected more, from the porters helping with the luggage to the waiter pouring coffee at the buffet. I found it unsettling, even as an American, where there's a strong tipping culture. I wonder how that felt to Australians, Dutch, Chinese, and others coming from places where tipping is not the norm.

We headed south the way we had come north: dusty roads edged by small buildings with grand names, fruit stands, paint stores, and countless places of worship. And an amazing array of spectacular gates.

Gates seem to be a thing in Kenya. Unlike the US, where

properties often merge seamlessly into each other, their corners subtly marked with inconspicuous pins and occasional orange ribbons, here, in Kenya, they believe in fences. Some are impressive, some not so much, but what they all have in common are the notable gates.

They are worked in metal and taller than a grown man, wide enough to let through a truck, and very ornate. Painted in bright colors and decorated with elaborate forged metal motifs, they appear to be status symbols rather than means to facilitate access, since I've even seen gates where the fence was missing. Just a monumental gate, standing alone to show the owner's worth.

We passed dozens of herds of lively goats, skinny cows, placid sheep, and even a few camels watched by tall men wrapped in blankets carrying large sticks. I asked Francis:

"Why does everyone carry a stick around here?"

"To herd the goats," he said.

"I get that. But some have sticks but no goats. Look at that one. Or that one."

I pointed to a few goatless men ambling casually along the road carrying long sticks and nothing else.

Francis shrugged.

"To help them walk?"

I didn't buy it. They looked young and healthy, and they weren't rope-walking. Is it just to have something in their hands? I wondered. The women were all loaded with stuff: babies tied to their back, bundles of wood, armfuls of hay, buckets of water, or at least bags of rice sitting precariously on their heads at jaunty gravity-defying angles. The men only had sticks.

Oh well. Another world mystery I won't solve, I thought, and I wondered if we'd ever get a potty break. Tank's eventful progress through the potholes had rearranged my insides, and the Kenyan coffee wanted out. As if he'd read my thoughts, Francis pulled into a large, fenced yard.

"Potty break. Good toilets, and you don't have to pay anything."

That was an odd thing to say, since we hadn't had to pay anything at any of the gas stations we'd stopped at before, but this was not a gas station. It looked like the world's largest curio shop, advertising handmade items they shipped everywhere in the world, and promising to accept credit cards.

The place was massive. We stepped into the Walmart-sized hangar packed with Maasai shields, lances, and blankets; sculpted giraffes, zebras, and warthogs from life-sized to thumb-sized; wicker platters and baskets; colorful paintings of elephants, lions, and women with pots on their heads; plus enough beaded necklaces and bracelets to blanket the whole of Kenya with some left over for Somalia. A smiling man delighted to meet us led us on the long and winding road from the door to the toilets.

"Jambo. Welcome," he said. "Everything here is handmade. Not machine."

"Oh," I said, wishing he'd pick up the pace.

"We ship anywhere in the world," he said proudly.

I nodded.

"That's nice. Toilets?" I asked.

"We also take credit cards," he said, just in case I hadn't noticed the half a dozen posters mentioning that.

"Great," I said, diving into the toilet and wishing we'd stopped at a gas station instead.

He was waiting by the door as I came out.

"Everything is handmade," he said.

I had not yet forgotten. I wanted nothing, but now that I had used his toilet without paying, I felt obliged to buy something. Oh well. I'll buy someone a gift, I thought, and looked around for something. I picked a mouse-sized warthog carved in wood out of its army of brothers and turned it upside down, looking for the price. It wasn't there.

"Oops. You touch, you buy," Steve chortled.

I refrained from throwing the warthog at his head and sat it back with the others as the man brought me a large basket to help me shop.

"We have all sorts of wood. Mahogany, acacia, even bone," he said proudly.

"I see."

"Stone too. And bone. Everything handmade in the back. Not machine."

"Very nice. But what you don't seem to have are prices. Out of these million things, I don't see a single one with a price."

"I'll help you with the price, don't worry."

"I bet you will. But that's not how we do it at home. I know we're not at home, but I find that difficult."

"Don't worry, I help you," he said. But I worried.

I know everything is negotiable, but I'd like to at least know where to start. In the US, Canada, Australia, New Zealand, Japan, and anywhere in Europe, everything has a price. Even in the Thai markets. You might negotiate with the vendor, and it's lots of fun, but at least you know where you start. Here? Nothing. You start in the darkness and stay there. Bad enough that I can't convert Kenyan shillings into dollars — or even Thai baht — fast enough to figure out if the candy bar I want to buy is 20 cents or 20 dollars. But this man expects me to fill a basket with stuff that I don't need and have no room to carry, then haggle on a wholesale price for everything. Who do you think gets fried on this one?

I smiled politely and walked up and down the narrow trail between sculpted elephants, painted lions, and metal-forged rhinos, looking for an elegant way out. I could just hand him a hundred shillings to pay for using his toilet, but I'd be insulting him by dismissing his merchandise. I could buy something small and pay whatever he wanted, but I'd feel taken. I am sure Francis brought us here on purpose — he probably gets his cut — and I know the man maintains those toilets for a reason: they are the bait to have cars stop, and then, once you use them, you feel obliged to buy. And he'll make sure you buy more.

I was in a bind.

I hate being ungrateful, but I hate being manipulated even more. No can do. So I smiled, thanked him, and handed back the basket and a hundred shillings, then headed to the car where Francis was conspicuously missing.

I climbed in just as a jeep full of tourists stopped by. Six haggard people poured out, crossing their legs as they looked for the toilets.

"Jambo. Welcome," the vendor said.

CHAPTER 20
OL PEJETA

THE ROAD to Ol Pejeta turned out to be the worst one yet. It was so bad that Francis drove Tank along one ditch, then along the other, to avoid the potholes big enough to swallow a car that afflicted both lanes. Dust rose like fog, goats bleated, and a pack of camels parked by the roadside blinked at us with sleepy eyes. A herd of mismatched cows of various sizes, persuasions, and colors, some sporting humps and some without but all fashionably slim and crowned with 2-foot-long horns stood by the fence chewing their cud. A bunch of women carrying babies on their backs brought them buckets of water. I watched it all and kept my mouth shut to avoid biting my tongue, and hoped my loosened joints would resume normal function when we stopped. Then a lone zebra ambled by, staring longingly at the fence, and I couldn't resist.

"What's she doing here?" I asked.

Francis pointed to the fence.

"That's Ol Pejeta. The zebra jumped out and now he wants back in."

No wonder. I wanted in too. By the time we rolled into the park, my eyes were gritty and I was choking with dust. But before long, the terrible dusty desolation outside turned into a wide grassy plain sprinkled with zebras, gazelles, and warthogs. I'd never seen so many zebras in one place. No wonder they didn't notice one missing. Showing off their striped pajamas, they looked well-fed and content and were having the time of their lives. Steve, who in only three days has turned into a pro with our new camera (so much so that I no longer bother to grab my iPhone) endeavored to take pictures. But, even though Francis stopped whenever we asked — albeit very slowly — between Tank's resounding vibrations and the animals always on the move, taking pictures was a challenge.

"I have never seen so many zebra asses," Steve declared.

He was right. No matter what they were doing or where we came from, every time he took a picture of the zebras, he ended up immortalizing their shapely behinds. They have an uncanny knack for that, just like kids who stop smiling as soon as you pick up the camera.

Two stallions, one striped in black and one in brown, had some issue to settle. They went at it hard, and everyone else gave them a wide berth. They circled each other, snorting, stomping, and rising clouds of dust, then bared their teeth to bite each other's throats. When that failed, Brown changed tactics. He tried to bite off Black's family jewels, but Black leaped aside and he missed. He tried again, but Black gave him a hard kick. They stopped to breathe for a moment, then switched. Black went after Brown's family jewels while Black kicked.

"Why are their stripes different colors?" I asked.

"The young ones are lighter. They darken as they mature," Francis said, and he took off without letting us watch the end of the battle. He drove across the sunburned plains with brownish tall grass, passing by hundreds of grazing antelopes, zebras, and gazelles that paid us no mind. Then, suddenly, they all rose their heads to stare in one direction.

"Lion," Francis said.

"Where?"

"In the grass. Where they are looking."

Sure enough, the grasses moved. A large head appeared, then a lion's back, the precise orange-brown of the grass. Before I could grab my phone, which was useless, anyhow, since we were too far, the lion had vanished. Nothing but the moving grasses proved he'd ever been there, and seconds later, that was over.

"They're impossible to see in the grass."

Francis nodded.

"That's how they hunt. They lie in the grass and stalk their prey until it gets close enough, then they attack. They always go for the slow — the weak, the old, and the very young. And even then, only one hunt in four is successful."

The gazelles kept watching the place the lion had vanished from, but we drove away. We passed dark water buffalos, their big horns so heavy they pull their heads towards the ground; we saw some new antelopes: large ox-like elands, and a few nimble springboks, who are the most successful of the desert antelopes. They don't need to drink, since they extract all the moisture they need from their food, and they can sprint up to 60 mph and jump 6 feet high to warn others of the looming danger. The spry springboks gave their name to the South African rugby team. Have you seen the movie *Invictus*? If not, you should. It's directed by Clint Eastwood and features Morgan Freeman in top form and Matt Damon. And great rugby — what's not to love?

Here, at Ol Pejeta, we finally saw rhinos, which are so weird they seem fake. Like armored hippos with two long curved horns sprouting from their nose, they seem to live to be seen. They sleep on their side, roll on their other side to sleep some more, then stand to graze, shuffling on their thick short legs until they get tired and lie down to sleep some more. What a boring life! That may be why there's so few of them left.

Rhinos are not small. At 16 feet long and 3500 pounds, they're monumental, if not pretty. Since they lack front teeth, they pluck their greens with their lips. For added glamor, they sport extra-thick skin and one to three curved horns, up to 4-feet-long, in the center of their forehead.

The main reasons rhinos are poached are their horns, which are much sought on the black market. Traditional Chinese medicine practitioners grind them and blend them into a plethora of potions and lotions that are supposed to cure everything, from fevers to nosebleeds and from baldness to impotence. But in fact, rhino horns are made from keratin, just like our hair and nails, and they have no proven therapeutic benefits.

Much to my surprise, I discovered that the two remaining African rhino species, the white and the black, are neither white nor black. They are both slate gray. The way to tell them apart is the shape of their mouths: the whites have wide lips adapted for grazing, whereas the blacks have a beaky mouth to better pick foliage.

The white rhinos furthermore divide into two subspecies: the southern white rhinos and the northern white rhinos. At over 20,000 extant members, the southern white rhinos are doing OK and are the largest rhino club on the planet.

The northern white rhinos are not. They're basically extinct, since they're all dead except for two females. Najin and Fatu are living their last days getting pampered at Ol Pejeta. The last northern white male rhino, Sudan, died ten years ago, practically bringing an end to the species.

Najin and Fatu are living the good life. They have their private enclosure at Ol Pejeta, and you need to book ahead of time for the privilege of watching them sleep, graze, and then sleep some more. We hadn't booked, but we were lucky enough to pass by their fence as they grazed nearby, so we got to see them and snap some pictures. I studied them closely, and I must confess I was disappointed they didn't look any different from the other dozens of rhinos we had just passed.

And, just between you and me, they aren't that pretty. At over 3000 pounds each, they're seriously chubby, so don't let anyone tell you that going vegan is enough to lose weight. They have a large hump that supports their heavy heads, and unlike unicorns, they have not one, but two curved horns in the middle of their forehead, a thick gray skin, and a surfeit of body hair.

They must have a nice personality, you say. Think again. This is what Fatu's CV says. It's posted right next to her enclosure.

"Fatu, born 2000 from Najin and Saut.

She has a rather bad temper and can be somewhat unpredictable. If piqued, she will show sudden aggression and won't take any nonsense from anyone. Nevertheless, she has a good rapport with her caretaker, and a belly and ear rub bring her back to good humor.

She loves sleeping in ditches with her snout resting on the ground next to her mother, Najin. They both enjoy the company of Tawa, the southern white rhino they live with. She's also very fond of cars and loves inspecting them at close range."

Her mother, however, sounds easier to hang out with:

"Najin, born 1989 from Nasima and Sudan.

"Najin takes after her father, Sudan. She is quiet, relaxed, adores tummy rubs, and often rolls on her back to enjoy them properly. She also likes mud baths but isn't very good at them because her legs won't allow her to sink properly.

She is accommodating and welcoming and she never minds

who comes close to her. However, she is easily startled by loud bangs and becomes dangerous when scared.

She can be quite pushy and knows how to get what she wants. She likes sleeping on soft ground and will lie down, letting off booming snores. She has been known to pass wind at impressive volumes."

After getting our fill of Najin and Fatu, we drove to the rhino graveyard, where the last white northern rhinos, including Sudan, rest under white commemorative plaques shaded by an old tree. A touching end to their story, I thought.

Before heading to our tent for the night, we stopped to visit Baraka, a blind black rhino who lives alone. We were lucky enough to talk to him, feed him carrots, and pet him, and his keeper told us his story.

Years ago, Baraka lost an eye while fighting another rhino, then lost the second eye to an infection. In order to protect him, he was moved to a special enclosure where he lives alone. He loves visitors who come to feed and pet him, so he had a hard time during Covid, when nobody came. But now that the guests and the carrots are back, he's quite content with his life.

It was easy to see that the young ranger was devoted to the rhinos. He had been looking after Baraka for over two years, and for other rhinos even longer, so he knew everything there was to know about them. He told us there is still hope for the northern white rhinos:

"The vets collected eggs from the remaining two females and sent them to France, where they already had frozen sperm from the last male. They created 29 embryos that will be sent to be implanted in surrogate white southern rhino mothers. If it works, it would be the first time that a species was brought back from the brink of extinction."

Exciting news, indeed. But not as exciting as Francis had when we returned to Tank.

"Hurry up. Someone saw lions. Let's go."

CHAPTER 21
THE FIRST LIONS

Lions!?!

Francis took off, riding the potholes like they were mustangs and leaving behind a cloud of dust. The wind whooshed, whirred, and whistled through the open car, going through my fleece like through macrame. Ol Pejeta is right on the equator — there's even a plaque showing you where it passes, though the burnished brown grass on both sides looks exactly the same. So does the weather, even though it's winter in the northern hemisphere and summer in the southern one. But at an altitude of 6000 feet, it doesn't feel equatorial at all.

That's when it started raining.

That might sound like nothing to you, especially if you're from one of those places like the Pacific Northwest or Alaska where rain is a way of life, but here in Africa it's a big deal. It hasn't rained in months, as witnessed by the burned grass and the thick clouds of dust the cars leave behind. And it's not supposed to, for months and months. But the weather is no longer like it used to be, so a rich equatorial rain broke over Ol Pejeta.

Francis drove like a daredevil, following trails only he

could see in search of the elusive lions, but the big cats were MIA. I was half-frozen, soaked to the skin, and mildly hopeless when he said, "There they are."

He was right. On a long naked ridge overlooking a waterhole, not one, not two, but five lions — all female — snored peacefully, completely unfazed by the eager tourists gawking at them from five packed safari vehicles. Cameras snapped, flashes flashed, people giggled with excitement, and the rain poured on as the lions slept undisturbed.

We joined the gawkers. I grabbed the binoculars and Steve got the camera, but between the rain and the impending dusk, it was getting too dark for pictures. Still, Steve performed his magic and caught them on camera just as they started raising their sleepy heads to look around.

"What the...?" the first one growled.

The second one cracked open an eye, looking disgusted.

"It's raining. It must be March," she grumbled.

The third one got up and shook.

"This is ridiculous. Let's go find some shelter."

"No way. Did you see the paparazzi? By tomorrow, we'll have our pictures all over TikTok and Facebook. Maybe even X. We're about to become famous. I always hoped to be a celeb someday," Second sighed.

"I don't want to be on X. I hate that musky guy," Third hissed, but she lay back between the others, measuring us with narrowed eyes. She licked her lips.

"How do you think they taste?" she asked.

"Like chicken. They all taste like chicken," First said.

"No way. These are canned. They might taste like sardines."

"Phew. I hate fish. And they stink of DEET," Fourth snorted, then got to her paws and took off behind the ridge.

The others looked wistfully behind her.

"Where do you think He is?" Fifth asked.

"I bet he polished off the rest of that impala we caught yesterday. As if he didn't eat half of it before we even got a taste."

"Oh well. He's our husband and the King." Third sighed.

Second gave her a dirty look.

"I hope he chokes on a bone," she roared, and departed. The others followed.

We were soaked to the bone, camera and iPhones included, when we headed back to our camp, following the other safari vehicles that threw mud at us. Minutes later, we dashed from the car like a couple of overfed senior gazelles, braving the pouring rain in search of our faraway tent.

Unfortunately, a well-intended helper planted an open umbrella in Steve's hand. That meant that besides jumping over puddles and shielding my iPhone from the rain, I had to watch my eyes. Despite his multiple talents, Steve is not skilled with umbrellas. In his hands, even the best-behaved umbrella will turn into a many-spiked monster intent on gauging out your eyes while pouring cold water down your back. All in all, that made for a most exciting journey, and not a short one either, but we made it back with all the eyes accounted for. We trudged up the uneven wooden steps to our porch and unzipped the heavy canvas with clumsy fingers numb with cold. I ripped the wet umbrella from Steve's hands just before he dragged it inside, and I dropped it on the porch. We were home.

Which brings me to telling you about our camp. Sweetwaters Serena Camp is an old hunting camp sitting by a waterhole inside the Ol Pejeta conservancy. It features a tree planted by Edward, Prince of Wales, in 1930, and another planted by the previous Crown Prince of Japan, who has since been promoted. The central buildings comprise a restaurant and a cozy sitting room reminiscent of an old-fashioned gentlemen's club. The tents, as they call them, are scattered around a waterhole where water buffaloes, gazelles, warthogs, birds, and the occasional rhino enjoy their sundowners.

The "tents" are sturdy buildings with substantial foundations and porches overlooking the waterhole. The generous bedrooms are furnished like rustic hotel rooms minus the modern embellishments. There's a kettle, a few rustic chairs, screened windows that zip up, and nice toiletries. There's also a bathroom with a shower and a toilet, but no door, so you'll get to know your roommate really well. There is no phone and no TV, but the power works full time, and we even have internet in the rooms, which is a first on this trip.

The tall pile of blankets surprised us. So did the gentleman who came bringing hot water bottles to warm our bed, but by the morning, we understood. The nights can get bitterly cold at 6000 feet, even at the equator, so the covers came in handy.

When the rain finally stopped, I journeyed back to the restaurant for dinner. Steve was too tired to come, so I let him play with the camera and download the day's pictures while I stumbled through the mud in the dark, hoping I'd meet no more lions that evening.

But the clean air smelled like rain, the birds sang like they were competing on *The Voice*, and the food, served buffet-style, was light on protein but heavy on Indian flavors and delicious. People enjoyed drinks by the fireplace, talking about their day and showing off their pictures, keeping me from feeling lonely.

I raided the buffet and tried everything, like I always do — I can't be trusted at all-you-can-eat buffets. I then stole a couple of dinner rolls, stuffed them with cheese for Steve, and headed back. That was the end of day three and Ol Pejeta. Tomorrow we're off to Lake Nakuru.

CHAPTER 22
THE CHIMPS

BUT WE CAN'T GO ANYWHERE before I tell you about the chimps.

The chimpanzee refuge at Ol Pejeta is an oddity. Chimpanzees are not native to Kenya, so for all intents and purposes, they have no business being here. And still, they are. How? It's a story.

In 1993, when a chimp rescue center in Burundi had to close because of the civil war, an agreement between the Ol Pejeta Conservancy, the Kenya Wildlife Service, and the Jane Goodall Institute established the Sweetwaters Chimpanzee Sanctuary in order to provide lifelong refuge to orphaned and abused chimpanzees from West and Central Africa. They now shelter 35 of them.

Newcomers are first nursed back to health, then introduced to one of the two groups living in vast natural enclosures divided by a river. They spend their days exploring, climbing trees and socializing, and sleep in indoor enclosures, each in their own nest, except for the mothers with young babies.

Problems often arise, our guiding ranger explained as he introduced us to the chimps. We didn't exactly shake hands with them, since they were behind a double fence we weren't allowed near, but he called them by name, producing the most authentic-sounding chimp calls, and then told us about them while throwing them handfuls of peanuts to keep them around.

That very morning, some elephants looking for greener pastures had broken into the other chimp group's territory. They had destroyed the fence, so we couldn't go visit. I wondered how — and if — they recovered the chimps, because I'm sure they took off.

In the wild, chimpanzees live in groups of fifteen to a hundred, but they often separate to travel, forage, or hunt. They use leaves to drink water and tools to gather honey and termites, and they sharpen sticks to hunt mammals, including other primates. They even eat specific plants to self-medicate for ailments like intestinal worms.

Chimp groups are strictly male dominated. Males patrol the boundaries of their territory and may launch violent raids on neighboring groups. Different communities often have unique customs, like specific grooming rituals or signals, similar to human dialects.

Of course life is different here at Ol Pejeta, where food and shelter are easy to come by and there's not much room to roam, but the dominant male still bosses everyone and prevents the other males from mating with any of the females.

"That's why the others have to masturbate," the ranger explains with strange glee in his eyes. "He's the only one to mate with them, so we have to give them contraception. We are not a breeding facility, and our resources are limited, so pregnancies are not wanted," he says.

"What sort of contraception do you use?" I ask.

"They implant something in the females' arms. But, since no contraception is 100 percent foolproof, we had four unexpected pregnancies."

I can't help but wonder why, instead of implanting these apparently ineffective devices in all the females, they don't perform a vasectomy on the dominant male, since he's the only one with access to the females.

But that's not the only problem with chimp romance. Males bully the females into mating with them using violence. They will bite, hit, and even injure them severely if they resist.

After an eight-month gestation, the female gives birth to a newborn whose only skill is clinging to mom. At six months, he learns to ride on mom's back. At two years, he starts exploring and interacting with others, but he still remains close to mom. By four, he is weaned, and he reaches puberty by nine. Chimps live around fifteen years in the wild. Since they live in trees, their major predator (other than humans) is the leopard, who is a skilled climber.

We watch them leap from branch to branch like acrobats, then jump to the ground to look for peanuts, walking on their short hind legs and supporting themselves with their knuckles.

"They prefer fruit, but they'll eat leaves and seeds too. Also honey, insects, and eggs. Even birds and animals, if they can catch them," the ranger says, throwing them another handful of peanuts.

We humans and chimps are closely related and share almost 99 percent of our DNA. We also share a lot of parasites and microbes and thus suffer from the same diseases, like HIV, malaria, Ebola, TB, and a propensity for dirty politics.

After hanging out together and grooming each other, male chimps associate in coalitions to dominate the group. A politically astute chimp might challenge a larger male and become dominant with the help of his friends. But, just like in humans, chimps' political alliances are fickle. Low-ranking males will often switch sides, because group instability is ripe with opportunities. In the chimp world, like in ours, being a sweet-talker and a back-scratcher will get you far.

Chimpanzees communicate by facial expressions, postures, and sounds. Happy chimps grin; moody ones pout and sneer. Macho chimps swagger and make themselves look bigger. To communicate at a distance, they pummel trees with their hands and feet — a process called drumming — or holler in pant-hoots starting with soft hoos and climaxing into loud screams and barks.

Just like us, they like to watch themselves in the mirror, laugh when tickled, and mourn when they lose someone they love.

Our similarities are the reason chimps are used for research, including inoculation with infectious agents and invasive surgeries, and many chimps were bred specifically for HIV research. Ham, a chimpanzee, flew into space. His 1961 mission aboard the Mercury-Redstone 2 spacecraft helped test life-support systems for humans, advancing space exploration. He returned safely and retired at a sanctuary after his mission.

Still, chimpanzee research continues to be controversial. Some argue that chimps should not be used for research, or they should be regarded as persons and subjected to the same ethical guidelines as humans unable to give consent. Others believe that all animals should be treated humanely, no matter if they're chimpanzees, dogs, or mice.

Our current understanding of chimps is based on Jane Goodall's extensive field studies. She was the first to point out how similar chimps and humans are in their attitudes and behaviors. Still, that does not make them human. Chimps are animals, and they are dangerous. There are multiple documented cases of chimpanzees snatching and eating human babies, and even adults aren't necessarily safe. Travis, a fourteen-year-old chimp who starred in several TV shows, lived with a family that treated him as their son. Still, one day he mauled a family friend, blinded her, and ate part of her face before getting shot by police.

Chimpanzees are endangered because of poaching, habitat loss, and disease. Their habitats were narrowed by deforestation and fragmented by road building, putting them in conflict with the farmers whose crops they threaten. They are still hunted for bushmeat, and their young babies are stolen for the pet trade.

I left the chimps with a mixture of uncomfortable feelings. I do feel for their plight, but I can't help but wonder what sort of humans we would be if we evolved from wolves instead of apes. We might value teamwork and loyalty above individualism and getting ahead. Our world might be less urbanized and more communal, with more respect for nature and a focus on living together. But we'll never know, will we?

For now, we're off to Lake Nakuru.

CHAPTER 23
LAKE NAKURU

THE TRIP to Lake Nakuru wasn't short. Not easy either, with more potholes than I could count and more tourist traps baited with toilets. But, five hours later and a tad worse for the wear, we looked over the lake's blue waters and the pelicans blanketing its shores like snow.

We expected flamingoes, but somewhere along the way, the delivery went wrong and the pelicans took over. The massive flocks of pelicans crammed along the shore opened their long yellow beaks to squabble. The floppy yellow bags hanging under their beaks looked nothing like the flamingo's gracious s-shaped necks. But, to keep with tradition, they were pink. Not Barbie-pink, mind you, just a cherry-blossom blush. Still, they looked like no other pelicans I had ever seen.

The long trip through the park to the Nakuru Sopa Lodge, our home for the night, was shaky and dusty. It was another 30+ kilometer mad rush to catch lunch, followed by a delicious buffet washed down with a cold beer for hydration. Our "tent," like the others, was a substantial modern building standing on the edge of a hill overlooking Nakuru Village and the park, a good quarter mile away from the central buildings, so we took the shuttle — a string of golf carts carting tourists and their luggage to and from their lodgings along a winding steep road. By the time we made it to our room — a large modern bedroom with a lovely view, a massive bathroom, and mosquito nets over the beds, but no TV or internet — it was time to get back for our afternoon drive.

Still, we took advantage of the hot water to do a bit of urgent laundry. Because of unforeseen circumstances (as in, I didn't pack enough of them), my socks were taking on a life of their own. Thanks to the ubiquitous red dust, my shirt had forgotten its original color, and I was almost as well camouflaged as the lions. But the shower would have to wait. Another mad dash to the central building and off we went for our game drive.

Speaking of it, even though I endorse the term drive — there's lots of that involved — I would dispute the term game. There's not much playing involved. It's more of a survival contest: the animals fight to survive the draught and each other, while we struggle to survive the drives. It's exhilarating and fun, but also oddly exhausting. We're both active people who don't sit around much, but we're utterly exhausted at the end of each day.

The drive took a while. It was a long way through red dust from the lodge to the open plains where the animals roamed. On the way, we met a ranger in camouflage carrying a rifle almost as big as himself. Francis stopped to chat and give him some water before we moved on. Steve worried.

"I don't like that he's alone. The poachers won't be alone if he meets them."

"But he has a gun. And probably a radio. He can get help."

Steve shook his head.

"I hope he uses his radio before his gun. So many rangers die."

He was right. About 150 rangers die each year protecting wildlife and their habitat, according to the Thin Green Line (TGL) Foundation, an international charity supporting rangers and their orphaned families. Poachers account for most ranger deaths on the job; the rest are caused by the hazardous environment and dangerous animals.

According to the WWF, 82 percent of African rangers have faced a life-threatening situation in the line of duty. Many feel threatened even at home, because rangers and poachers often belong to the same community. Seventy-five percent of rangers had neighbors threaten them over their work.

We wished the young ranger the very best and went on our way. We saw hundreds of well-fed zebras swishing their tails and nodding as they walked as if they were listening to Michael Jackson. We also met some jolly plump warthogs, uglier than sin, who always have a smile on their faces and kneel to eat.

"Why do they do that?" I asked Francis.

"To reach their food," Steve said.

"But look at that one. He's not kneeling, and he can still reach his food."

"Then it's to pray before dinner," Steve said.

"So why isn't the other one praying?"

"He's an agnostic."

We saw dozens of placid water buffaloes, hundreds of agile impalas and gazelles, and countless quarrelsome baboons. We even saw a tiny plane surrounded by curious zebras, a dozen giraffes, and a convention of self-impressed marabou storks dressed like bald funeral directors. But what we were really looking for, Francis said, were leopards. And there were none.

"Watch those trees by the water. That's where they like to hide," Francis said.

We watched and watched, but we saw nothing but colorful birds. Then something moved in the bush. An ugly red head with a terrible haircut ending a long, powerful neck leaned forward from a sloped rump. A second later, it was gone.

"A hyena," I blurted.

Francis looked unconvinced.

"Where?"

I pointed to nothing but the grass. He shrugged and moved on.

It was getting late, and I was getting tired when he got a radio signal that got him excited.

"There's something to see, but it's far away. We'll have to go fast."

Fast we went, leaving behind a cloud of red dust and clenching our teeth to prevent them from cutting off our tongues. We found a row of safari vehicles whose occupants, packed like sardines, stared through binoculars at something. I stared too, but I saw nothing but the grass.

"Lions," Francis said.

"Where?"

He pointed to where everyone stared, but there was nothing. I wondered if they were all delusional when I finally saw them in the grass: a pride of lions, all asleep. Some on their side, some on their back, piled all over each other like a litter of young puppies full of milk. A tail swished here, a leg moved there. Someone rolled from one side to the other. An ear flicked, then a head came up for a moment.

"A male,' Francis said, then counted to seven.

I don't know how. I could see nothing but lion parts, and I didn't know what belonged to whom. But I did count four tails.

We waited for a while, but nothing happened, so I looked around to see who else was there. A hundred feet across the road, a lone hyena gnawed on something, watched by two gloomy vultures glaring at her with greedy eyes. Were those the lions' leftovers?

A de-fleshed ribcage sat by the side of the road. There was no meat left, just bloody ribs and the spine of what might have been a gazelle. Whatever it was, it had been enough to feed a pride of lions with leftovers for the hyena and the vultures. A sad reminder that in the savanna, someone has to die so that others can live.

Like most Americans, I buy my meat from the supermarket, all sanitized and wrapped in plastic, and bearing no resemblance to the living creature it came from. Killing to eat is not pleasant to admit to. We dislike it so much that we disassociate our food from the living animal it came from: flesh becomes meat, cows become beef, pigs become pork, sheep become mutton.

But, since they have no supermarket and no credit cards, lions, hyenas, and their kind have no room for these sensibilities. They must hunt and kill to survive.

Would I want to witness a kill? I would not. Even seeing it on TV turns my stomach, and I'd rather look away. But I won't, because ignoring others' suffering doesn't make it disappear. I owe that gazelle the respect of recognizing that her death, one of many, kept those lions alive. And, while gazelles, zebras, and wildebeest are still countless, lions, leopards, and cheetahs are not. The predators' numbers dwindle every day, and most of them are endangered. Thanks to that dead gazelle, a lion cub might survive.

CHAPTER 24
HEADING TO THE MAASAI MARA

DAY FIVE TURNED INTO A DOOZY. On our way back from seeing the lions last night, I asked Francis, like I always do, about tomorrow's plan. I don't know about you, but I always have a Plan A, a Plan B, and usually a Plan C. Plan D is somewhat optional.

"We're getting up early, having breakfast, then heading to Maasai Mara." Francis said, narrowly avoiding a pothole.

Say what? That couldn't be right. I knew for sure we were staying in Nakuru for two nights. That's why we'd dragged all our bags from the car and scattered everything all over the room. We even did laundry, for God's sake!

He was right. I had somehow added a nonexistent day to Lake Nakuru, and the time had come to take it out.

"It's a long drive, a good five hours, so we need to get going early. We're having breakfast, then leaving at 7:30," Francis said.

"Eight?" I pleaded. I could leave at five, since I'm always up by three to do my writing for the day, but breakfast doesn't start before 6:30. By the time we eat and check out, we won't even have time to return to our remote room to get our luggage.

Francis shook his head.

"Seven-thirty. We don't want to miss lunch."

That we don't. We don't maintain figures like ours by missing meals. Seven-thirty will have to do.

We decided to get up at five, get ready, pack, and drag the luggage with us for breakfast. Not an exciting proposition, but the only one I could think about. This should work.

I didn't count on the power cut. And the rain.

Since 2:30, when I woke up, the power has been off, with brief returns when everything plugged in clicks and sparkles for a moment only to disappear again. It's pitch dark, and I can hear it raining over the laundry we did yesterday. And, since I didn't expect this, I didn't dig out our flashlights, so I operate by the light of my iPhone. Packing should be fun, I think, and decide to wait for the power to return before waking Steve.

At 5:15, the phones ding and the lights click, signaling the return of the power. It's still pitch dark outside, so we can't see how badly it rained on our laundry.

It did. Not a little, but a lot, as we discover when we have to wring it as best we can and pack it in a side pocket to keep the rest of our clothes from getting wet. The rain keeps falling like it's going out of style as we ride the golf cart uphill, drenching us and our luggage.

After a big buffet breakfast with the usual spread, we check out, drop another $50 in the well-marked tip box, and we're on our way

The rain cleaned the air and melted the dust. It also turned the terrible park roads into muddy skating rinks. We slide, skid, and splash as we leave behind the Nakuru Sopa lodge to rush towards the famous Maasai Mara.

"I thought this was the dry season," I say, keeping my tongue out of the way of my chattering teeth and tucking my hands in my armpits to warm them.

"It used to be," Francis says, narrowly missing a wet water buck who materialized out of nowhere to stare at us, blinking out the rain, "but the weather changed a lot. We get more rain than we used to, even when we don't expect it."

"Good. Most of these places look like they can use it," I say, looking at the brown grass and stunted bushes.

Once out of the park, the trip southwest to the Maasai Mara isn't bad, especially if you nap through a couple hours of potholes. The farther south we go, the bigger the buildings, the fatter the cows, and the larger the herds. People look different too. Women still carry children on their backs and all sorts of things in their arms while the men wave sticks, but they all look more relaxed and more content. I think I even saw someone smile.

"People seem more relaxed down here," I remark.

Francis shrugs.

"Sure. You're more relaxed when you have money," he says.

It turns out that tourism brought the Maasai a new prosperity. With remarkable foresight, they changed some of their traditional ways, and it paid off. From the ferocious lion hunters whose rite of passage was killing a lion single-handed, they remodeled themselves into guides and wildlife protectors. They leased their lands to conservationists, creating wide areas where wildlife is protected, but they still can graze their cows while deriving a substantial income from the land and the jobs thus created. They work as guides, drivers, wildlife guardians, and whatever else the tourism industry demands.

"They put all their wealth in cows," Francis says. "They have a lot of cows."

They sure do, as we notice when we hook a right on some terrible dirt road that seems to go nowhere and find ourselves surrounded by a gazillion cows. Guarded by tall men wrapped in red checkered blankets carrying — you guessed it — sticks, the cows hang out like they're waiting for the bus. They loiter in groups of a few dozen that go as far as I can see, doing nothing.

They look better than the cows up north, where you could count every rib and the hollows in their pelvis were deep enough to hold water. These cows aren't fat either, but they are sleek and shiny, with large humps, long curved horns and soft eyes. Unlike American cows, with their docked horns and udders so heavy they hang to the ground, these cows seem udderless. You have to look hard to see who's a girl and who's a boy.

"What is this?" I ask Francis, pointing at the sea of cows.

"Cows," he remarks observantly.

"Thanks. But what are they doing here?"

"Just waiting."

"For what?"

"To get in."

"In what?"

"In the park."

Now that's a set of visitors I hadn't counted on. I didn't even realize cows were into tourism.

"What do they do in the park?"

"They graze."

It turns out that part of the Maasai's arrangement is that they can graze their cows in the park's protected area, but only at night. From 6 p.m. to 6 a.m., thousands of cows roam the park, bonding with the antelopes, the gazelles, and the water buffalo and filling with grass. Still, like bovine Cinderellas, they must vanish before the tourists drive in. Any cow disrespecting this schedule will get impounded and locked into a pen, and must pay a stiff fine before getting released on the recognizance of her owner. It's a neat arrangement — the tourists get their zebras and giraffes, the cows get their grass, and the Maasai get their money. I wonder what the lions get.

We finally reach the park gate. Francis leaves us waiting in Tank and goes to pay for the entrance. We're checking our phones as two bald Maasai women wrapped in red blankets, their ears hanging low with earrings and their arms heavy with beaded necklaces and bracelets, stop by and stare at us through the windows.

"Welcome," one says.

"Thank you."

"Where are you from?"

"America."

"Oh, America! Look!"

The woman shows me the dozen necklaces in her right hand.

"No, thank you," I say.

"No, thank you!?! But look!"

She shows me the dozen in her left hand. They look the same to me, but what do I know? I haven't worn a necklace in ages. I feel well dressed if I have clean socks.

"No, thank you."

She frowns to tell me I'm not behaving properly. She shows me a handful of wood-carved warthogs.

"Look."

I must admit I'm partial to warthogs — they're so ugly, they're cute, and they always have a smile on their faces, even when they rush to gore you. But our condo has a strict no pets policy.

"No, thank you," I say.

"No, thank you," she repeats in utter astonishment. She pulls out her last trick — a wooden platter with a painted giraffe.

"No, thank you," I say, and break eye contact. I scroll on my phone to let her know I've had enough. She hasn't.

She knocks on the window.

"What's your name?"

I keep scrolling as she keeps knocking and probably cursing me in Swahili. It doesn't feel good, but I resist the urge to tell her to go away. This is her country, after all.

But I won't buy things I neither need nor want. And if you think I'm heartless, think again. We paid — a lot — for the privilege of being here. The park entry alone is $200 per person per night, without counting the lodging, the food, the car, the guides, and the endless tips. All that to buy extra cows!

She finally gives up and moves to Steve. The other lady has been working on him for a while, but he's no more partial to necklaces than I am, so she didn't get far. With the corner of my eye, I watch to see if he gets sucked into buying some bracelets or at least a giraffe, but he keeps his nose in his phone.

It feels like forever until they give up.

But they don't. Not really. Like a couple of homing pigeons, they converge on Francis, who's finally returning from the booth. They demand he buy something. It takes him a while to shake them off, but he finally squeezes into Tank and starts the engine.

"Welcome to the Maasai Mara."

CHAPTER 25
THE MAASAI MARA

The Maasai Mara's Fig Tree camp must have seen better days. Like the other lodges, it has a central building comprising the reception, the restaurant, and of course, the souvenir store, and a string of so-called tents lining the river. It also has a temperamental generator that takes frequent breaks, keeping you in the dark from midnight to 4 a.m. plus a few hours during the day, a tight schedule for hot showers, and a limping internet at the central building, only when the power is on. But it has something none other had: hippos.

When we finally made it to our tent after having checked in, listened to the obligatory briefing, and enjoyed a tasty but rather challenging buffet lunch where I couldn't recognize half the offerings, we were shocked to discover a pile of bloated bodies lying on a little beach across the river, less than a hundred feet from our tent. Mass murder[1] I thought, and got all excited, but it turned out to be something even more thrilling. Packed like sardines, the resident hippos were taking their afternoon nap. Once in a while, someone snorted or shook his head. But most sunbathed and snored, unperturbed, while a handful of birds traveling up and down their bodies picked at their pests and gave them a nice massage.

We would have loved to linger and watch them, but as always, we were in a hurry. So we headed back to the parking lot where Francis and Tank waited to take us on our afternoon drive.

We headed out on incredibly muddy trails that put Tank and Francis to the test. I'm glad to say they both passed, though a few vehicles behind us were forced to turn around. We skidded our way through the mud alongside burnished plains scattered with zebras, water buffaloes, gazelles of all kinds — I still can't keep them straight — and a variety of antelopes. A new one, the topi, deserves special mention for its sleek figure, glossy skin, and the brown blotches on its shoulders, knees, and shapely behind that look like tattoos. A lone hyena slept in the bushes, then another, which made me wonder. I thought they lived in clans? What's with all these shady characters hanging out by themselves?

Just as the sharp cold rain restarted, soaking us to the skin and making us wish we'd stayed in the camp to watch the hippos, we fell upon a dozen safari vehicles, all facing in the same direction. We've learned by now that when things all face the same way — whether they're safari vehicles, gazelles, or birds — you'd better believe there's something worth seeing. So we headed there in a hurry.

"Lion," Francis said, pointing to a dark blotch in the grass. He stopped behind the other dozen vehicles as Steve grabbed his camera and elbowed me out of his way. I grabbed the binoculars. A dark-maned lion in dire need of a haircut lay in the grass to our right, about 20 feet away. His eyes were narrowed and his nose wrinkled like those of a cat caught in a downpour. He didn't seem to like the rain, and I had to agree.

I watched him getting rained on for a while, then I looked around to see if there was anything more exciting.

"Steve."

Steve, busy taking pictures, ignored me.

"Steve."

Nothing.

I shook him.

"What?" he barked.

I pointed straight ahead. A bunch of lions blocked the path ahead of us. They were almost under our wheels, surrounded by safari vehicles. There must have been a dozen, all female except for a couple of young males with light, short manes, and they seemed totally unfazed by the attention. They lay in the mud, blinking out the rain and cursing climate change in lion language.

"Oh," Steve said, and turned to them.

Ten minutes later, he was still taking pictures when one of the females stood, yawned, stretched, and passed through the gap between the safari vehicles into the grasses to our left like she didn't have a care in the world. A couple minutes later, another one followed, then another. Before you could finish chewing one of the tenacious pork ribs I had had for lunch, all the females had moved to our left, leaving behind the two young males and Simba, their lord and master, who dozed in the rain like he'd been working night shifts in the ER.

They didn't go far — 50 feet maybe — before plopping in the tall grass.

I was wondering what that was about when I noticed the topis.

A few hundred feet to our left, a herd of topis — a couple dozen, maybe — stood frozen, staring at us. Why? I wondered. We'd passed by them so many times before and they didn't grace us with a glance. Now, they looked positively entranced with us, though we were stuck in the mud. Sharp as I am, I finally got it: they weren't staring at us. They were watching the lions.

The lionesses had fanned out in the tall grasses. Between the thick rain and their burned-grass color, they were so well camouflaged that I could only distinguish the dark back of their ears — unless they moved. They'd spread apart, getting ready to ambush the topis, but the antelopes were not close, and they were watching.

Far left and far right, the grasses moved. Two lionesses had snuck forward, while the others stayed put, keeping the topis' attention.

For a while nothing happened, other than the rain falling harder and harder. When Francis could no longer stand seeing Tank getting soaked, he squeezed in the back through the opening between the front seats and pulled down the pop-top. Quite an accomplishment, I must admit, since the space was narrow, and Francis is not a small man.

All of a sudden, the leftmost topi turned away. With slow, stiff steps, he moved away from the others.

The lions pricked their ears. We gawked.

Two more steps. Three.

The air crackled with excitement.

"What's going on?" I asked Francis.

"The topis feel the lions but can't see them, so they don't take off for fear of running straight at them. The lions are still too far, so they're waiting for the ones who snuck closer to give the signal."

The first topi stepped further.

"That's the one they'll go after," Francis said. "Moving away from the herd makes him vulnerable."

What on earth is that topi thinking, I wondered, when he suddenly kicked his hooves and took off at a gallop. The others followed a moment later. Minutes later, they were just tiny brown spots far away.

The hunt had failed.

Simba, who had been lying in the grass all this time like this wasn't his problem, got to his feet. He shook his wet, tangled mane, and with slow, heavy steps, crossed the road just inches from us. A few feet later, he dropped to the ground between the lionesses.

The females converged around him, dragging their muddy paws. I watched their (mostly) silent conversation.

"Whose project was this? Marjorie, was it yours?"

Marjorie shook her head in disgust, spraying water over everyone else.

"Initially, it was my idea, but then Georgina said we should fan out early…"

Georgina flicked her tail in annoyance.

"I said let's go undercover. Did you think the topis were so stupid they'd wait for us to just waltz in there?"

"They're stupid enough. And if we had gotten a bit closer..."

"That's enough! The topis are gone, it rains like it's March, we're soaked to the skin, and there's no dinner. Whose fault is this?" Simba roared.

Instead of cowering, the lionesses stepped forward to confront him.

"Your fault, you lazy bum. You lie there doing nothing while we do all the work, and then you expect to eat first. Why don't you get off your butt and come to help, for once? Then we might all get something to eat."

Simba snorted in annoyance. Not only was he hungry and wetter than a drowned kitten, but the debriefing hadn't gone as planned.

"You females don't know your place anymore," he roared, then turned tail and left.

The trip back was more exciting than usual. Untangling the traffic jam we were in took half an hour, then a vehicle got stuck in the mud and blocked the road. Someone pulled him out, but he had forgotten to lock his back doors, so they kept swinging open, making a ruckus and threatening to mow anyone who got close. By the time we got back, we were just as wet and hungry as the lions. But at least our dinner was waiting.

To learn more about lions, read the next chapter, On Lions. Or skip it and move on.

CHAPTER 26
ON LIONS

JUST LOOK AT A LION, and you'll see why he's the king of the jungle. They are powerful, majestic animals, and they're completely unruffled by all the attention they receive, even though nobody but elephants and Taylor Swift cause so much giddy excitement in onlookers.

The average lion's 600 pounds of weight comprises 60 percent muscle, some innards and bones, and less than 14 percent fat. That's even higher than the muscle percentage of a cheetah or a professional bodybuilder, who both reach up to 50 percent of their body weight. The only animal that's even more ripped than the lion is the tiger, who can reach up to 70 percent muscle and 7.7 percent fat. For comparison, a whale is 40 percent fat, a polar bear almost 50 percent, and to my surprise, a sumo wrestler only 25 percent. I had never thought of them as being skinny.

The male's mane, his most distinctive feature, grows downwards and backwards to cover his head, neck, and chest. The mane starts growing as the lion enters adolescence and it reaches full size at age four. The sexiest males — a.k.a. the most dominant — have the darkest, thickest manes, which go with higher testosterone levels. Besides being a marker of strength, manes protect lions during fights, giving the best endowed males a survival advantage, but they also make them more sensitive to heat.

Few white lions are left in the wild. Most were captured in the 1970s and bred to produce trophies for canned hunts, thus depleting the gene pool in the wild. A canned hunt is the killing of an animal kept in an enclosure to simplify a trophy hunter's job and guarantee his success.

Free lions nap for about twenty hours a day, like cats. They socialize and groom after dusk, and they usually hunt at dawn. They may walk for a couple of hours a day, and, if they're lucky, they will eat for almost an hour.

Lions are the most social big cats. They live in prides of fifteen to thirty individuals that include a few related females with their cubs and one or more adult males we'll call Simbas. The females are the pride's stable core, and they do not tolerate new female intruders. When they grow, the females remain in their birth pride, but the young males leave to look for an unrelated pride to join.

Shunned bachelors travel widely and spend years as nomads, surviving harsh conditions and scavenging or hunting alone or in pairs. They are critical to the species' survival by ensuring genetic diversity when they eventually take over a pride.

Larger prides control better hunting territories with abundant water, prey, and shelter, like river confluences. Males and females spray urine to mark their territory and defend their range against intruders together.

Lions are apex predators, so they have few natural enemies besides humans. They prey on zebras, wildebeest, and warthogs while avoiding adult elephants, rhinoceri, and hippopotami. They are crucial in maintaining the ecosystem's balance by controlling herbivore populations. Without them, overgrazing could devastate grasslands and deplete water resources.

A hunt's success depends on how many lions take part. A single lion hunting in daylight will get its prey less than one time in five, but a larger group might be successful up to a third of the time. Their night vision, much better than ours, allows them to hunt in low light, giving them an advantage over prey less adapted to nocturnal activity.

The young start stalking prey at three months, but they don't hunt until one year, and don't become proficient until two. A lone lion can bring down a zebra or a wildebeest. Larger prides can even hunt baby elephants, but males rarely bother to hunt. Getting dinner is the females' job. They hunt as a pack, and, like football players they each have their favorite position, whether it's stalking prey on the "wing" before attacking or defending the center in case dinner tries to flee.

Lions can sprint up to 40 mph, but only for brief bursts, so they need to get close to their prey before charging. They stalk at night or under cover, waiting to dart until they're close. With their last leap, they down the prey and kill it with a clamping bite to the muzzle or throat.

Lions squabble over kills when food is scarce, and young cubs are the first ones to suffer. But when there's enough food, everyone gets their fill, even the old and the crippled. An adult needs 10 to 15 pounds of meat a day, but it can eat up to 70 pounds at one sitting, then rest and eat some more.

Lions are not ashamed to scavenge, and they'll keep an eye on vultures whose circling might signal a potential dinner. Most of the carrion lions eat is hunted by hyenas. Lions tend to ignore hyenas unless they are feeding, in which case they try to force them away from their kill. This also works the other way. A clan of hyenas may force a lion off his kill. But lions and hyenas may tussle even if there's no food at stake, and hyena clans may mob lions in their ranges and kill their cubs.

Lions dominate cheetahs, leopards, and wild dogs. Whenever they can, they steal their kills and slaughter their cubs. To avoid them, cheetahs hunt during the day, and leopards hide their kills up in tree branches. Lions occasionally fall prey to crocodiles, as evidenced by the lions' claws found in crocodiles' stomachs.

Lionesses reproduce by age four. After a gestation of 110 days, the female hides in a den to give birth to one to four spotted cubs weighing around 4 pounds each. The cubs crawl the day after birth, they open their eyes at one week, and they walk at around three weeks. While the cubs are helpless, the mother hunts alone, staying close to the den and moving them often to protect them.

She brings them back to her pride when they're seven weeks old and they can socialize and play with others. Lion cubs get weaned after six months and they reach maturity around three, when the young males leave the pride. The tuft at the end of their tail appears around five, and they start aging at twelve.

After ousting a pride's previous male, the new males will kill the young cubs to force the females into estrus. The females try hard to defend them, but they are seldom successful. Lion cubs are also preyed upon by leopards, hyenas, and wild dogs.

Lions can live up to seventeen, since adults have no natural predators to cull the weak and the sick. That's why they suffer from ticks and parasites, including tapeworms they ingest in antelope meat.

Lions talk. A LOT. They growl, snarl, meow, purr, puff, bleat, and hum, and their deep roars can be heard from many miles away. They socialize by rubbing their heads and licking each other like cats, especially on the head and neck where they can't lick themselves.

Lions are classified as vulnerable from a conservation standpoint. Conservation strategies are targeted at reducing the fragmentation of their habitat, maintaining a sufficient wild prey base, and avoiding conflicts with humans.

That's why herders are encouraged to keep their cattle in enclosures, but that's difficult for the Maasai, whose traditional livelihood depends on nomadic pasturing, and whose traditional rite of passage to adulthood is killing a lion single-handedly.

Cash revenue from tourists and the new job opportunities have convinced some elders to discourage lion hunts, but the lions' numbers are still declining.

CHAPTER 27
OUR HIPPOS

I'VE ALWAYS BEEN an animal lover. Ever since I can remember, I've never met an animal I didn't want to take home, much to my mother's chagrin. (Those were the old times when we used to walk to school, played hide-and-seek in the cemetery, and explored dilapidated places our parents didn't know existed.) I returned from wherever I had been two hours late, scratched and covered in mud, and carrying some bird with a broken wing, a lizard without his tail, or a litter of one-day-old puppies some jerk had dropped in the street. But I never brought home a hippo.

Most likely because I never found one. Still, I confess I never thought of hippos as being cute, endearing, or social. I saw them over and over at the zoo, and even on TV, staring at me with their round eyes engulfed in fat, bloated and wading on thick, short legs. They looked neither friendly nor pretty. But our hippo neighbors changed my mind.

They were fast asleep when we'd seen them at noon, but now, at sundown, they frolicked in the muddy water like a bunch of kindergartners at recess. They sank, then resurfaced to push and shove each other, snorting and flicking their ears, touching their noses and spurting water up high. Nine were bluish-gray, but one was skin-pink and easy to distinguish. After watching them for a while, I decided that Pink and Medium Gray had something going on.

They touched noses and snorted, gazing in each other's eyes, then bumped heads and snorted again before submerging, only to start over. I was still trying to figure out whether this was romance or rivalry when one mooed. The other mooed louder. A second later, Pink dove underwater to resurface under Medium's belly, throwing him off his feet. Blurting and groaning, they chased each other, bumping into everyone else. Water sprayed, mud splashed, and the river boiled with playing hippos until they got tired and moved to playing peek-a-boo.

Everyone sank, then came back up until only their bulbous eyes floated above the muddy water like disembodied organs. They stayed put, staring at each other until they had to breathe, then brought up their round nostrils and snorted, spraying water all around, then sank again and started over.

Half an hour later, they found a new game: Who can open their mouth wider and roar the loudest? The patriarch, the largest one, opened a mouth large enough to swallow a compact car and roared like an incoming freight train. A baby hippo tried to imitate him. He stuck his head out and opened his mouth as big as he could, then squealed like a piglet. His father chortled and showed him how it's done. The baby tried again. Much amused, the patriarch demonstrated again, roaring until our tent started shaking. The other ones got into the game, and before long, the river bubbled with roaring hippos, their mouths open so wide I worried they'd dislocate their jaws.

They kept at it for a while until Pink got tired. She climbed out of the water on the little beach they'd slept on, and shook. Two more followed, and they started chasing each other on the ground with the grace of drunk sumo wrestlers, until they got tired and fell asleep.

We sat on our tiny porch watching them until dusk turned into dark and the mosquitos came out for dinner. We went back inside behind the screens, but Steve was so entranced he stood by the door to watch them some more.

It was pitch dark when we returned from dinner, but we could hear them snorting, barking and groaning until late in the night. This morning, they had started again before five, waking up the entire neighborhood. But not us. We were up early, since day six was to be different: We'd take off with the light and have breakfast after we returned.

The park's rules are strict: no safari vehicles on the trails before six thirty in the morning or after six in the evening, under fear of severe punishment. Not sure what the punishment is, but seeing that they not only impound but also fine the cows, I wasn't that eager to find out.

That's why Tank was just one of the dozen vehicles revving their engines in the parking lot at 6:29. They were all raring to go, especially the balloon people, who have a special dispensation to get on their way at 5:30 but got stopped by the rain.

Which brings me to some other safari offerings I haven't yet mentioned. For only $450, you can take a balloon ride over the plains of the Maasai Mara and enjoy the savanna from above. You wake up before dawn and ride to a ridge where the air currents are suitable to launch balloons. You wait until the carefully controlled burners fill the balloon with hot air, then hop into a basket the size of a small elevator with your new fifteen close friends and wait for the hot air to lift the balloon — and the basket — above the ground. Before long, you float with the wind, watching the earth drift below and enjoying the sunrise. After about an hour of relishing in the exhilarating views and excessive togetherness, you hopefully land where the safari vehicles are waiting with a luxurious champagne breakfast, having taken oodles of pictures and made the memories of a lifetime.

It's nice, if it's your thing and you can afford it. We skipped it, since we'd already done it in Turkey. It was during Covid, and even though the views were fabulous, the forced intimacy with so many strangers was a bit much.

For only thirty dollars, you can book a trip to visit a Maasai village to chat with the Maasai, visit their abodes and learn about their lives. You may watch, and even join, their traditional dance, which involves jumping as high as possible, again and again, if you're a man, and undulating your charms until your necklaces take on a life of their own, if you're a lady.

That sounded interesting, but from what I had read, it becomes a massive shopping trap you can't escape. You are kept there until you buy stuff, whether or not you like it, so we skipped that too.

For extra entertainment during your safari, you can also book a variety of massages and facials at American prices, shop in the ubiquitous curio shops, and drink adult drinks at the bars present at every establishment. Some places — like the Fig Tree — even feature a folkloric Maasai show after dinner, with locals in native attire presenting their songs and dances. All in all, there's no shortage of things to keep you entertained, the food is plentiful and mostly good, and the people are friendly and obliging. But truth be told, we aren't here for the food or entertainment. We came to see and learn about Kenya's wildlife and her people, and that's what we will do. Read On Hippos to learn more about these fascinating creatures, or skip and move on.

CHAPTER 28
ON HIPPOS

UNLIKE ANY OF our other animal friends, the hippopotamus (plural hippopotamuses, hippopotami, or easier, hippos) is not terrestrial, but semiaquatic. As fitting for his name, which means "river horse" in Greek, he spends his days sleeping in the water to stay cool, and his nights foraging for greenery, and that's not easy, since he needs a lot of greens to maintain his impressive physique. At 3000 pounds and 20 feet long, hippos are the largest land mammals after elephants and rhinos. Also the most dangerous, causing more human deaths than any animal but the mosquito.

Despite his porcine looks, the hippo's closest relatives are dolphins and whales with which he shares a common ancestor. Unlike his aquatic cousins, the hippo can't swim, but he walks underwater, holding his breath for up to five minutes, and can run up to 20 mph on land.

Hippos live in pods, a.k.a. bloats, comprising one bull and five to thirty cows and calves. They inhabit rivers, lakes, and mangrove swamps, where they have lots of grass and water deep enough to immerse themselves in. At night, they forage on land, traveling up to three miles to graze a hundred pounds of grass.

Males are territorial in water, where they claim a stretch of up to 300 feet, but not so much on land. The bull breeds with all the cows in his territory but will allow the young bulls to stay unless they challenge him.

To mark their territory, hippos poop and spin their tails to spread their feces in the hippo version of "poop hitting the fan." They threaten each other by yawning. They open wide their massive jaws to almost 180 degrees to show off the 20-inch incisors they sharpen by rubbing against each other. They save them for fighting, since they grasp their food with their lips and grind it with their molar teeth.

At 2000 pounds per square inch, a hippo's bite force is even higher than that of a lion or a tiger, allowing him to crush bones and even split crocodiles in half when his calves are threatened.

Hippos call each other with a "wheeze honk," a high-pitched yell that morphs into a deep call both friends and foes can recognize from afar. To broadcast their presence, they hold their heads at water level and send a signal that travels far through both water and air.

Females stop growing around 25, but males grow throughout their lives, up to 50 years old. Their dense bones are adapted to their enormous weight, and their weight lets them sink and walk along the water's bottom. They don't float, because despite their chubby appearance, hippos are mostly muscle and two-inch-thick skin with little fat. Their eyes, ears, and nostrils sit high on their skull to stay above the water even when the body is submerged.

Hippos secrete a reddish, oily substance that acts as a natural sunscreen and antibacterial. This "blood sweat" protects them from UV rays and infection, which is essential to living in muddy, stagnant water.

Cows become mature at six and males after seven. They mate in the water, with the submerged cow coming out to take a breath every few minutes. After an eight-month-long gestation, she hides to give birth to a hundred-pound calf. She lies on her side to nurse him, and carries him on her back in deep water to bring him to her pod when he's a little older.

Hippo calves are much sought after by crocodiles, lions, and spotted hyenas. That's why they are kept in nurseries well-guarded by adults. They suckle until they're one year old.

Hippos love their spa, when they lie in shallow water and let barbell fish clean them of ticks and parasites. Those intrepid hygienists even clean their teeth when hippos open their mouths to invite them in. Hippos also employ the same red-billed oxpeckers who pamper rhinos, impalas, and giraffes. The crafty birds land on their backs and pick up their ticks, dead skin, and even their earwax.

From a conservation standpoint, hippos are classified as vulnerable and endangered. Their major threats are losing access to fresh water and poaching. Unfortunately, hippo meat is considered a delicacy in Africa, and their teeth are used to replace ivory. The decline of their habitat forces them to raid farms and puts them in conflict with humans.

Still, while Africa's hippos are threatened, Columbia has more than it wants. The four escaped pet hippos of the Columbian drug lord Pablo Escobar multiplied to over a hundred. Their unchecked growth threatens the native ecosystems because they out-compete native species, erode riverbanks, and alter aquatic habitats. Efforts to control their population, including sterilization, are ongoing.

CHAPTER 29
DAWN SAFARI

Our dawn safari started with a light drizzle and roads — if you can call them that — even worse than the day before. It was so cold that Francis didn't want to pop up Tank's top, so we took off through the mud, following the balloon vehicles.

The whole savanna reeked of manure, but there was no cow in sight. Only graceful gazelles, grazing with their ears pricked and watchful eyes looking everywhere; placid water buffaloes chewing their cud, their hairy black heads burdened by massive horns; and countless zebras showing off their shapely striped behinds like they always do. That's why we started calling them zebrasses.

It looked like an uneventful morning other than Francis's spectacular driving skills and the balloons rising up slowly in the pink sky behind us until we saw the lions.

They were two, both adult males, and, contrary to everything I'd learned about lions, they were together. They came towards us from the grasses to our right, crossed the road right in front of Tank, stopped for a muddy eye-opener from the ditches, then ambled majestically towards the river to our left. They couldn't care less about us — but that's not new. Other than a silly teenage elephant here and there, nobody here pays us more attention than they would a weight loss commercial. But they barely glanced at the smattering of gazelles and topis watching their every movement with worried eyes. The boys weren't there to hunt. Unhurried and relaxed, they acted like they were headed to the club for a game of squash and a cigar, and the antelopes knew it. None of them moved an inch, and I wondered: How do they know? How do they know when the predators — lions, hyenas, and such — seek food, and when they're just going about their daily business?

We passed a lone jackal, a handsome animal much like a wolf, with intelligent watchful eyes, tawny gray fur, and a fluffy tail, then met a drenched hyena. Everyone was wet, us included — there was no other way to be in this deluge. And this is the dry season. I'd hate to see it when it really rains. But that hyena looked particularly pissed, and I wondered why until I saw the cubs.

There were two, only feet away. Nestled in the tall grass by the side of the road, they resembled stuffed teddy bears with their round ears, curious eyes, and spotted fur so fluffy it looked like feathers. Their mom had stepped away from them to distract us. Soaked, all alone, and worried about her cubs, she was so miserable she looked pitiful, but that's the last thing they are. Hyenas are the only creatures in the savanna, other than humans, who can defeat a lion, steal his kill, and kill his cubs. They are cunning, fierce, and ruthless, and unlike any of the other predators, their business is thriving. While the number of lions, leopards, and cheetahs are plunging, the hyenas stay strong. How come? To learn, read the next chapter: On Hyenas.

We drudged on, splashing from pothole into pothole between wet antelopes and zebrasses, when Francis detected a gathering of safari vehicles on a ridge far away. "Hold on," he said, and stood on the accelerator, propelling Tank into a frenzy of swerves, glides, and splashes. Our hearts were racing by the time we got there. When we saw the show, they raced even faster.

Lying in the thrashed grass, a pride of lions enjoyed their supper. Big Simba, his massive head crowned by a brown tangled mane, crinkled his big muzzle and growled like a Harley-Davidson to deter his almost-grown cubs from devouring his dinner, but he was having no luck. Whatever they ate, I couldn't see under the swarm of muscular bodies fighting over it, but no amount of growling would deter them. Mouth near mouth and nose next to nose, they pulled, ripped, shredded, and chewed on whatever Simba held between his paws. He struggled to hold on to it, but it was like holding water between your fingers. His dinner was vanishing bit by bit.

A few feet away from the fray, a forlorn young male watched them from the corner of his eye, hoping there'd be something left for him, but the chances looked slim. Too old to be treated like a cub, too young to have his own pride, he hung around hoping for scraps.

The young lioness next to him had managed to steal a black hoof attached to a long, skinny leg. It looked like nothing but skin and bones, but she industriously chewed on it, extracting whatever little food it still had. A few hundred feet away, on top of a hill, six lionesses, who must have hunted the kill, stood hungry in the rain.

"Is this the same pride we saw yesterday?" I asked Francis.

He nodded.

"Ninety percent yes. The big lion, the young lion, and the bunch of big cubs. And the lionesses up on the hill."

It looked like the debriefing had helped, after all. After yesterday's failure, today's hunt had been a success, though not a big one. The swarm of lions wrestled and shifted, and for a brief moment, I saw what must have started as a warthog.

Barely an amuse-bouche for this pack of hungry diners. And, by the looks of it, those who had done the work reaped none of the reward.

I didn't know whether to feel sorry for the lionesses, pity the hungry young male, or mourn the poor warthog, when a deafening roar brought my eyes back to the swarm. A particularly stubborn cub had ripped out a bone with some flesh from the kill and had stepped away from the fray to munch on her prize. Big Simba was not pleased.

He roared, but he didn't let go of his dinner to chase her. Seeing her success, the others took heart and tried to do the same. Like dogs fighting over a toy, they sank their teeth into the prey, trying to drag it away from their father. But Big Simba had had it. He roared again, then lifted a heavy, clawed paw and slapped one of the youths, leaving a bloody gash on her forehead.

She stepped back and sat, blinking in the driving rain, just feet away from the food, and watched the others fight over it without complaining.

A rolling thunder covered the ruckus, then another. A bolt of lightning split the sky, and the rain came down harder.

Simba stood and stepped back, pulling the carcass away, but the cubs held on. There were four of them, all big, heavy, and hungry. So he sighed and dropped back to eat what he could.

Not much was left of that warthog by the time we moved on. It was cold, wet, and dark, and, as Steve said, we already knew what the outcome would be. When there was nothing left but the bones, the young lion may get his chance for a snack, unless the hyenas and vultures chased him away. But the one thing certain was that nobody would go to bed with a full belly tonight.

We passed by the hungry lionesses lying in the rain on the

ridge. They looked sodden and seriously irked, and I could almost hear them talk.

"Whose bright idea was this? Let's get a warthog, you said. They're stupid and easy to catch. And look at us now. We won't get one bit out of him, I tell you. Not one bit."

"Shut up, Marjorie. Go pound mud or something. I don't remember you saying no when I suggested it. And after yesterday's debacle, you have no room to talk."

"Well, at least we didn't get a debriefing," one mused, flicking her tail to shake away some water.

"Oh, Mavis, you and your freaking silver lining. You know what that means, don't you?"

"What?"

"We'll have to go hunt again. In the freaking rain. On an empty stomach," Marjorie roared.

"Well, the rain will hide us. And the empty stomach makes us lighter."

Marjorie shook her head in disgust, spraying water over everybody else, and growled something sounding like: "dumb bitch."

"So, what do you want to hunt this time? The topis are too fast, the warthogs too small..."

"How about a zebra? They're so fat they can't run fast. And one of those fat-arsed convicts should have enough meat for us all."

"A zebra? Are you nuts? Those things kick like mules. One hoof, and bye-bye teeth."

"Maybe we could find a lame one?"

I don't know what they decided, but I hope they had better luck. Still, statistics say that less than 30 percent of lion hunts are successful, and even then, a kill doesn't always mean a meal. Life in the savanna is tough. For someone to live, someone else has to die.

CHAPTER 30
ON SPOTTED HYENAS

WITH FEW EXCEPTIONS, most safari goers are there to see the Big Five. That's what they brag about over dinner, on Facebook, and in their reviews. "We saw all Big Five within 24 hours of arrival!" "It took us a few days, but we got to see all the Big Five!" Or: "Sadly, we never got to see all the Big Five, but it was still a great safari."

What the heck are the Big Five? I wondered.

It turns out that "The Big Five" is a term stolen from hunting, referring to the five major trophies big game hunters most chase: lion, elephant, leopard, rhinoceros, and water buffalo. These are supposedly the hardest animals to hunt on foot.

To borrow its cachet of danger, excitement, and triumph, and thus attract tourist business, travel companies, safari outfits, and guides stole it for today's photographic safaris. But, since we don't shoot rifles, only cameras, and we're never on foot but ensconced in the safe cocoon of our safari vehicles and we're barely allowed to touch the ground, I will argue that the idea is obsolete.

Silly too. While I agree that lions and elephants are intriguing and leopards hard to find, the water buffaloes, who do nothing but graze, glare, and poop, are about as intriguing as Holstein cows and far less pretty. And the rhinoceri who sleep most of the time are as exciting as CAT bulldozers that ran out of gas.

Thinking that the Big Five are the only animals worth seeing is also demeaning to other worthy, fascinating creatures, like the cheetahs, the giraffes, the dung beetles, and the hyenas.

As a response to The Big Five, some coined a few other interesting classifications:

The Little Five: The elephant shrew, the leopard tortoise, the red-billed buffalo weaver, the ant-lion, and the rhino beetle.

The Ugly Five: The vulture, the warthog, the marabou stork, the wildebeest, and the hyena.

When we came to Kenya, I knew, like everyone else, that the lion was the king of the savanna. Imagine my surprise when I discovered the savanna actually has a queen. It's the hyena, which is the only animal — other than man — that lions fear.

Although taxonomically feliforms (related to cats), hyenas act more like dogs. Like wolves and wild dogs, hyenas are excellent runners and can maintain 40 mph for miles. Unlike cats, big and small, that use their claws to grab their prey, hyenas catch it with their teeth. Their paws end in blunt, nonretractable claws that provide excellent traction while running and taking sharp turns. Despite that, their grooming, scent marking, and behavior are more similar to that of cats.

Hyenas are larger than wolves. They have long, powerful necks, massive torsos, and a distinctive stiff, sloped back because of their long forelegs and short hind legs. Like giraffes, they are easy to recognize from afar by their stance. Their fur looks scruffy, but they have a rich mane of long hair around their massive heads with large, round ears. Their jaws are powerful enough to crush bones up to 2.5 inches in diameter, making them essential for nutrient recycling in the savanna.

They eat so many bones their feces can turn white from the calcium, and they can kill prey with a bite to the neck without breaking the skin.

In spotted hyenas, females are larger and more aggressive than males. To make it even more confusing for researchers who struggled for ages to tell them apart, their external genitalia are shaped like a penis. Female hyenas mate, urinate, and give birth through this pseudo-penis which allows them to control who they mate with. They could even write their name in the snow if they found it.

After 110 days of gestation, the mother gives birth to two to four three-pound cubs through the long, inch-wide birth canal. The birth process is so difficult that 15 percent of first-time mothers and 60 percent of the first-born cubs do not survive. Why did they evolve to this difficult and dangerous anatomy? No one knows.

Hyena cubs are born with their eyes open, dark hair, and a full set of teeth. They get their spots in a few weeks and will spend nearly a year at their den site, nursed only by their mother. At six months, they head out to forage with the clan, but they continue to nurse for another year and remain close to mom until four. Lactating females can have up to a gallon of milk which is richer in fat and protein than that of any other terrestrial carnivore. One feeding can hold the cubs for up to three days, so Mom can hunt while an auntie watches the babies.

Spotted hyenas live in female-dominated clans led by a queen, and the clan hierarchy is so strict that a female's cubs inherit her rank, giving them priority access to food over lower-ranking males.

Unlike other predators, hyenas are unaffected by infectious diseases like anthrax, rabies, and distemper, thanks partly to their remarkable digestive system. Their gut is so short that bacteria have no time to multiply, and their gastric juices are so acidic they kill bacteria and dissolve bones.

Their antibody-rich blood helps keep them healthy. Interestingly, the number of antibodies in their blood depends on their position in the clan. The queen has the most, and the males have the least. That may be why females live twice as long as males.

Hyenas can't sweat, so they cool down by licking their forelegs and groom themselves like cats. Also like cats, they don't raise their legs to urinate but mark their territory with their anal glands.

Contrary to widespread beliefs, even though they scavenge and eat whatever they can get their paws on, from old carcasses to bugs, hyenas still hunt most of their food, usually medium and large prey like antelopes and gazelles. But unlike lions, who stalk their prey and then leap to grab it, hyenas wear down their prey in long chases. That's how they pick the weak, the wounded, and the slow, culling the sick animals and helping maintain herd health. Still, a clan won't hesitate to drive a lion off his kill, even though he can kill them with a paw stroke.

Spotted hyenas are VERY chatty. They whoop, grunt, groan, low, giggle, yell, growl, laugh, and whine, and they recognize each other's voice. They whoop and keep track of each other and coordinate while hunting. The nervous laugh they are famous for is actually a sign they feel threatened.

Hyenas rarely prey on humans, but the opposite is not true. In Saudi Arabia, Morocco, and Somalia, hyena meat is halal and considered a delicacy. They are also believed to have medicinal benefits. In Somalia, the hair of spotted hyenas is thought to increase self-control against adultery, and their teeth are worn as amulets for strength and endurance.

In Somalia, hyenas are used to cure mental illness, as described in this 2013 BBC article by Richard Hooper:

"There is a belief in my country that hyenas can see everything including the evil spirits people think cause mental illness. So in Mogadishu, you will find hyenas that have been brought from the bush and families will pay £350 to have their loved one locked in the room overnight with the animal."

"The expensive treatment — more than the average annual wage — is as brutal as it sounds. By clawing and biting at the patient, the hyena is thought to force the evil spirit out. Patients, including young children, have died during the process."

Despite that, and despite their habitat loss and fragmentation, hyenas are classified as "of least concern" from a conservation status. Aren't they remarkable creatures?

CHAPTER 31
THE LONG DAY

LIKE EVERYTHING past its new shine, the idea of spending a whole day slipping and sliding through mud and freezing our assets seemed less exciting today than it would have been a week ago. We got our fill of gazelles and antelopes, and even the elephants are no longer the thrill they used to be. By the way, if you, like me, don't know the difference between gazelles and antelopes, here it is: Gazelles are small, fast antelopes, but not all antelopes are gazelles. The oryx, the topi, the eland, the springbok, and even the wildebeest are antelopes but not gazelles.

We've seen countless warthogs, a bunch of hyenas and a few jackals, and we've met dozens of lions and giraffes.

"Is there a point to going the whole day and skipping lunch, rather than taking two short trips with a break in between?" I asked Francis.

I thought he'd jump on the opportunity — after all, that would mean less work for him. A couple of two-hour drives are less than one long eight-hour drive; even I knew that. Francis would have more time to do whatever he does when we don't drive, since we rarely see him outside our drives. Guides have their own quarters and their own table, which is only fair. That gives them a break from the job and from putting up with demanding customers like me peppering them with incessant questions like me.

"We can go much further, and we can see things we don't get to see so close to camp. I love it," he said.

That settled it.

After another abundant breakfast with omelets made to order and sausage and bacon and pastries and fruit, plus juices and cereal and whatever else you can think of, washed down with lots of excellent Kenyan coffee, we met Francis at the car. The seat next to him was occupied by a tower of cardboard boxes bearing the lodge's logo, so I got all excited that someone sent us a gift. But no.

"This is our lunch. We'll head towards the Mara River, cross it, and we'll get to the Tanzanian border and see the Serengeti. We'll check who's waiting for us around there, then return to camp about four to rest."

We approved of the plan and headed out bundled in all our clothes (did I mention it gets cold in Kenya?) and armed with our cameras and binoculars. We passed one Thompson's gazelle after another — I finally got to know them. They are small antelopes who can reach 55 mph, with sharp horns, dark-ringed eyes, a dark side stripe, and twitchy tails that never stop moving. We saw topis, their muscular brown bodies and orange legs with dark knees and shoulders looking tattooed shining in the sun, and then a remote elephant herd. The roads had dried somewhat, so we made better time, though the patches of deep water slowed us down every couple of minutes. Still, we were progressing nicely when Francis turned around.

"There's something to see."

He's always secretive like that, just in case we don't get to see it. Minutes later, we lined up behind three other safari vehicles whose occupants stared at something far away.

"What are they looking at?"

"Cheetah. See her?"

I looked and looked. I even grabbed the binoculars, but I still saw nothing.

"Right there, near the topi," Steve said.

I looked at the topi. Behind the topi. In front of the topi. Nothing but grass.

"Right there, between the topi and that enormous tree."

I traced the line between the topi and the tree. Three times. Nothing.

"How can you not see her? She's right there." Steve pointed at something 200 feet behind the topi. Oops. Another topi. Sure enough, all this time I'd been staring at the wrong antelope.

Twenty feet or so behind the correct topi, a lone spotted shape that could have been a cheetah, a spotted dog, or Paris Hilton sunbathing in her fur coat, watched the topi. The topi watched her back.

Then, with a recklessness I couldn't have fathomed, he headed in her direction. Step by step, he got so close he looked like he could touch her. She didn't move.

"Why did he do that?" anyone would have asked.

Not me.

"Why is she not eating him?" I asked.

"He's too big for a lone cheetah. And he's got sharp horns and hooves that could harm her badly. It wouldn't be the first time an antelope killed a cheetah, and she knows it."

Soon, the topi got bored and got back to his grass-mowing business, and we went our way.

As we got further and further from the camp, the grasses grew taller and thicker, and the animals fewer and fewer. Before long, we found ourselves crossing a sea of golden grasses I could hide in. It looked like paradise if you happened to be a herbivore. My personal idea of paradise would involve a sea of rare steaks "au poivre," with a few chocolate cakes thrown in for good measure. But we're not talking about me. We're talking about zebras, gazelles, and antelopes, and none of them were here.

"Why aren't there any animals?" I asked Francis.

"The grass is too deep. They can't see what's hiding in it, and they're afraid."

"But why is the grass so deep here, when it's so short by the camp?"

"Because of the soil. But this is what the Great Migration comes for. In June and July, millions of wildebeest and zebras come from Tanzania's Serengeti, cross the Sand River and the Mara and mow this to the ground. When they're done with it, they go back to return next year."

"How do Kenya and Tanzania work this out? Are there any problems?"

Francis shrugged.

"Not so good. In Tanzania, they light the savannah on fire to stop the migration and keep the tourists there. But the animals come anyway."

That shook me to the core. Burning the savannah, which is already spent, otherwise the animals wouldn't travel thousands of miles to find food, with all the risks that entails, to stop the migration, one of the seven wonders of the natural world? That's terrible. I got ready to fight.

"That awful. Is there something to do? Someone to complain to? Like environmental conservation, or something?"

"It doesn't help. They say they do it for land management, so nobody does anything."

I was still chewing on this thought when Francis listened to the radio and turned around.

"Something to see," he said, and took off.

In my sixty-plus years, I've never seen a more social human than Francis. Golden retrievers, yes. And maybe a couple of chocolate labs, but humans? No. Half of the time he's on the phone, which rings every five minutes, or on the radio, which chatters all the time, having brief conversations in Swahili that must be related to the job. Whenever we meet another safari vehicle, he pulls way left in the ditch to let them pass, but they seldom do. Nine of ten drivers stop for a word with him, and they're always black men with dazzling white smiles, some wrapped in red Maasai blankets. They exchange a few words and chuckles, then go about their business and we go about ours, better informed. That's how we know when there's something to see straight ahead and when there isn't, when the river is too deep to cross or when something worth seeing is happening somewhere. "I know this guy," should be Francis's motto.

"If you were a lady, your reputation would be in tatters," I said, the umpteenth time he told us he knew a guy. He laughed and moved on.

Before long, he hooked a left off-road to join three more safari vehicles up to their windows in grasses. And between them, trying to go about his daily business, was a leopard.

Leopards are not easy to see. Unlike lions, they don't spend their days lazing in the open field. They hide in trees to sleep, eat, and stalk their prey, and they're loners, unless they're mating or have young cubs. That's why finding a leopard was a big deal and got everyone excited.

Everyone but the leopard, that is. He glanced back at the half-dozen safari vehicles chock-full of people staring at him through microwave-sized cameras and kept going. He didn't run, but didn't loiter either. With a fluid, low gait, he vanished into the grasses in no time. The cars followed, and I worried they'd run him over, but the drivers were all cautious and experienced, so we found him again seconds later. He wasn't scared, but he wasn't loving it either. He took off again.

I felt bad about chasing him. The poor thing was like a celeb trying to escape the paparazzi — harassed, but hopeless. In humans, that's the price of fame. Here, in the Maasai Mara, it's the price animals have to pay for living in a protected habitat instead of being hunted. It's sad but true that without the tourists who spend their dollars to see the wildlife and fuel the local economy, the savanna would soon turn into maize fields and cow pastures. The big five, the little five, and the ugly five would be nothing but memories. As one of my professors used to say, there's no such thing as a free lunch.

For more on leopards, read: On Leopards. Or skip on.

CHAPTER 32
ON LEOPARDS

THE LONELIEST, stealthiest, and most elusive predator of the savannah is not easy to find. First, because he's nocturnal, so he's usually out and about when we aren't allowed to roam the parks, so we slumber under our mosquito nets. And second, because unlike humans sporting leopard prints, the leopard doesn't wear them to get noticed — just the opposite. Leopards' rosette patterns are so effective at camouflaging them they are nearly invisible in dense vegetation or dappled light, making them one of the hardest animals to spot in the wild. Black panthers are the same species, but they express a recessive gene, like white lions.

The leopard goes undercover to stalk his prey, since his dinner depends on his stealth; he hides from hyenas and lions, since meeting them might cost him his dinner and maybe even his life; and don't even get me going about poachers, a.k.a. humans.

That's why leopards love trees. To them, trees are safety — lions or hyenas can't reach them there. They provide a vantage point to stalk potential dinner, and may even be a hunting ground — leopards won't turn down a juicy monkey, should one become available. Trees are the pantry where they keep their kills to hide them from hungry scavengers, and even their own lazy teenagers who'd rather raid mom's fridge than hunt their dinner. So, if you're looking for leopards, check out the trees.

Leopards are sleek but muscular, with a large head, short legs, and a six-foot body ending in a strong, three-foot long, tail. Males weigh about 150 pounds, females a bit less.

Of all the savanna's predators, the leopards are the most complete athletes. While cheetahs are the sprinters, hyenas the long-distance runners, and lions the strongest, leopards can do it all and then some. They climb like cats, swim and hunt in the water, run at over 36 mph, leap over 20 feet, and jump up to 10 feet high.

They rely on their excellent vision and hearing to stalk their prey and approach within 20 feet before pouncing. They kill small prey with a bite to the neck and strangle larger prey, then drag even heavy antelopes up into their trees or caves to store them.

Leopards are solitary and territorial. Adults only associate to mate, but females will interact with their offspring even after weaning. A male's range may overlap with those of a few females, and the size of the range depends on the prey availability.

Leopards are mature at three, and will attract mates with a distinctive "sawing" call, resembling a saw cutting wood. Females seduce males by presenting themselves in suggestive positions when in estrus. Leopards' lovemaking is a tense, noisy affair that lasts a whole week. If you heard it, you might think you were listening to a deadly fight.

By the end, they're both exhausted, hungry, and thirsty, and pretty pleased to go their own ways and not see each other for another two years, when the female is ready to mate again.

After 100 days of gestation, she gives birth to two to four cubs weighing 1 to 2 pounds, usually in a cave or a thicket. They open their eyes at a week, start eating meat at nine weeks, and follow mom at three months. They stay with her for up to two years and remain close afterwards.

Still, most leopard cubs don't survive their first year. They fall prey to lions, spotted hyenas, and even other male leopards who will kill a female's cubs to bring her into heat.

Leopards live twelve to seventeen years, but they are a threatened species. Habitat fragmentation and deforestation to expand agriculture has increased conflicts with humans and leopard mortality rates. They also fall prey to poaching and trophy hunting.

Since leopards are already extinct in many African countries, Botswana banned leopard hunting. In eleven sub-Saharan countries, trading leopard skins and their body parts is restricted to less than 2,560 individuals each year.

That's still an awful lot of dead leopards, if you ask me.

CHAPTER 33
THE MARA TRIANGLE

WE LEFT the leopard to deal with the herds of paparazzi and went on our way. We drove and drove until the landscape changed again. The long golden grasses disappeared, replaced by short green ones, as we approached the thundering Mara River.

We heard it from afar, but seeing it was something else. I couldn't believe that two million wildebeests and zebras could swim across that angry, swollen, thundering mass of brown water dragging with it entire trees, roots and all. And still, they do. They come every year, braving everything that stands in their way: the intentional fires, the terrifying river, and the starving crocodiles that call the Mara home.

This year's unexpected rains bloated the river until it overflowed its edges, rising awfully close to the bridge. We crossed the shivering bridge with some trepidation, then stopped to stretch our legs and take a few pictures of the Vervet monkeys.

We visited the washrooms, which were clean and fitness-inducing, being the type that requires you to squat. In case you've never tried it, I can tell you that squatting over a latrine is easy, but getting back up when you're done is not, especially when you're not really keen on touching anything around you. Which brings me to a word of warning: If you're planning a safari and you're not fit, take a little time to build your endurance beforehand. No matter how luxurious the resort and how ubiquitous and friendly the help, there'll be unassisted squatting, whether at designated toilets or in the bush. There'll also be LOTS of standing in your safari vehicle if you want to see, especially if you're in a group and you have to wrestle for your view. Getting in and out of the tall safari vehicles or rocking boats requires flexibility, balance, and strength. There's also lots of walking up and down uneven trails, climbing steps and steep trails, and stumbling in the dark for your dinner.

We returned to Tank to find Francis chatting with a young man in uniform who introduced himself as Davis.

"Davis will take you for a walk to stretch your legs. He'll keep you safe," Francis said. "For a small tip."

"Of course," I said, wondering what that was all about, and what there was to see that we hadn't already. I figured that Francis just needed a break from us for whatever he was concocting, so we followed Davis, who stopped by the concrete box that was the checkpoint.

"Let me get something to protect you."

A stick, I thought, but one of his buddies handed him a large rifle. Oops. Davis grabbed it and off we went to cross the Mara bridge back to where we'd just come from.

"What are you protecting us from?" I asked.

"Animals can be dangerous. Elephants and lions. Also, poachers."

Elephants and lions I had seen, but I had yet seen no poachers that I knew of. "You have poachers here?"

He nodded and showed me his right hand. The index finger was shortened. It had been amputated at the level of the first phalanx, so two-thirds of it were missing. It was an old wound and well healed, but I couldn't help but wonder how he'd pull the trigger should the need arise.

"The poachers cut me. But I'm lucky I still have my job and I can work. I'm a border patrol, and I stop bad people from coming from Tanzania to kill our animals. We need them for the tourists," he said.

Interesting outlook. To him, poachers were not only bad, but also foreign. That contradicted my research that says that most rangers get threatened or killed by poachers belonging to their own community.

"You like your job?" I asked.

He nodded vigorously.

"I chose it," he said. "I was born here, I grew up here, and I work here. And I can earn enough to take care of my children."

He had four children, two boys and two girls, who lived with his wife outside the reservation. He went to see them for a week every month, and the trip cost 2000 shillings each way, which amounted to almost $30 for the round trip. Expensive, but worth it, he said.

He flashed a brilliant white smile when Steve slipped him a thousand shillings as a tip. It was worth it, even though I still don't know what we were supposed to see. It was lovely to learn about his life, but Francis and Tank were waiting, and off we went.

"Where are we going?"

"We're going to the Mara Triangle. We're not supposed to go there, since it's under different management, but I know this guy…" He waited for his guy to open the barrier keeping us out.

The Mara Triangle is the southwestern part of the Maasai Mara National Reserve, divided from the rest of it by the Mara River. This is where the Great Migration enters the Maasai Mara from the Serengeti, which makes it a prime location for this wildlife spectacle. It sports the same gazelles, antelopes, and elephants, but its roads are better, and the stunning landscape is dominated by odd-shaped cliffs rising over the rolling plains, the massive umbrella-like acacias elephants and giraffes treasure, and tiny green ponds covered in white and purple waterlilies. It was gorgeous and serene, and I was getting ready to relax and enjoy, when, after a quick radio chatter, Tank took off like a rocket.

"Cheetah," Francis said, and drove towards two safari vehicles whose tourists stared at something in the grass. I only saw a lone impala standing at attention at first, but the binoculars showed me the two cheetahs watching him from afar. They were almost the same orange as the grass as they sat next to each other with their backs towards us and their eyes glued to the impala who stared back.

For the longest time, nothing happened.

"What are they doing?" I asked. "Why isn't the impala running away? And why aren't the cheetahs attacking?"

"God didn't make gazelles that smart," Francis said. "And the cheetahs are too far. They can run fast, but only for a short distance, so they need to get closer before they try to attack."

The standoff lasted for a while; then the impala had enough. He broke into a run, then, a few hundred feet later, he stopped and looked around. He saw nothing, so he got back to his grazing.

But, unbeknownst to him, the cheetahs followed. Their spotted coats blended so well with the grass that I could only see the grass moving as they snuck behind a massive rock outcrop that hid them from the impala's view. Having forgotten all about them, the impala kept grazing and they slinked even closer. All of a sudden, the impala felt something and broke into the run of his life, but it was too late. The cheetahs followed.

They flew high through the air in effortless leaps. They

seemed to close in on him, but then they stopped making progress. It looked like the impala would just make it when a cheetah leaped once more. Water splashed. A strangled scream broke the silence, then everything went quiet. Even the grasses stopped moving, but it wasn't hard to imagine what went on, and it wasn't pretty.

A curious topi came to see what was going on. He gawked from afar, then stepped closer to watch the struggle, and I wanted to shout: Run away, you fool! But Francis was right. God didn't make antelopes that smart. He started grazing just feet away from the cheetahs, but fortunately, the cats had enough food for themselves and any cubs hiding in the brush, unless someone forced them off their kill.

"They'd better eat fast," Francis said. "Lions, hyenas, and vultures will steal their kill if they find them. And that brings us to our lunch."

The grass was too wet to sit outside, so we sat in the car and opened our cardboard boxes. It was an abundant and unexpectedly delicious cold lunch with a chicken stir fry, a toasted sandwich of roasted vegetables, a boiled egg, a bag of tomato-flavored chips, a banana, a yoghurt, a brownie, and a tiny box of mango juice. We ate our fill while chatting with Francis about his job.

As a young man, he used to work as a taxi driver in Mombasa. One day, someone asked him for a ride to one of the parks, and he loved it. He decided to change professions and started studying everything about wildlife. He bought books and took classes, and a few years later he started working as a guide. He's been doing it for twenty years and still loves it.

Covid hit the tourism industry hard. Things were dead for a couple of years, so he opened a shop in Mombasa.

"What did you sell?" I asked.

"Serials."

That got me thinking. How do you even sell serials? Like maybe cable subscriptions? Or Netflix? Magazines, maybe? But would you even sell those in a shop?

"What kind of serials?" I asked.

He shrugged.

"Whatever kind we could find. Mostly maize."

Steve choked on his brownie.

"Cereal," he said. "He was selling cereal."

I nodded like I knew that, and Francis went on. Tourism picked up again after Covid. After years of working as a freelancer, Francis now works full-time for a travel company. He's one of the ten guides, and only gets paid when he works, with no paid vacation, retirement benefits, or health insurance. Jobs get assigned preferentially to the guides that customers ask for by name after reading reviews, Francis said, but he didn't ask us to leave a review. His wife still lives in Mombasa and his kids are grown up.

We finished lunch and left half of it for dinner. In most camps, dinner doesn't start until 7:30, which is late for me. It usually involves a trip in the dark to the restaurant and back, and quite a bit of waiting around. The food is good, but it's so much hassle that I wouldn't mind packing it in early, since we have an early departure tomorrow. We're leaving the Maasai Mara to drive to Lake Naivasha, five hours away, and we have a scheduled boat ride before lunch.

We got ready to head back, but the long day's surprises weren't over. A quick radio chat, another U-turn, and we joined two safari vehicles watching two lions sunning themselves in the grass. An adult male, let's call him Simba, and an adult female — say, Ginny — lay in the grass, sleeping back-to-back, with no other lion in sight.

"They're on their honeymoon," Francis said. "When you see just one male and one female, it means she's in heat and they left the pride to mate. For an entire week, they don't hunt, they don't eat, they just mate again and again, every few minutes, up to fifty times a day."

Oh wow. Fifty times a day? That sounded like a lot. But what did I know about lions' honeymoon traditions? Or anyone else's, in fact. That sounded exciting, so we grabbed our cameras and got ready. But their clock seemed to be off. Fifteen minutes passed and nothing happened.

I looked at Francis. He nodded encouragingly.

"The female initiates the coupling. She wakes him up and seduces him and they mate," Francis said.

I wondered how she'd seduce him. Sexy lingerie seemed unlikely. I saw no makeup and smelled no perfume. Maybe she does some sexy dance? I wondered, looking forward to finding out. But Ginny failed to follow Francis's suggestions. She lay asleep, flicking her ears and tail once in a while to shake the flies, then fell back asleep.

Simba woke up. He lifted his head to glance around, no more impressed by our presence than if we'd been selling car insurance, then looked at Ginny and snorted.

She didn't move.

He rolled from one side to the other, then back, measuring her expectantly. She ignored him.

"Hey, Ginny," he purred like a well-oiled Harley Davidson.

She opened one eye.

"What?"

"You know…"

She snorted and closed the eye back.

He sniffed.

"Ginny?"

"What?"

He sighed and dropped back to the ground.

They were still snoring as an incautious jackal came to see

what was going on. Nothing was, but he couldn't have known it. If he looked for food, there wasn't any, and if he looked for trouble, there was plenty. He finally got it and skittered away, leaving the lions to their snoozing.

More cars arrived. Dozens of eyes watched for the nonexistent foreplay, but the lions were not impressed.

"We'll wait a few more minutes, then head home," Francis said. "We have a long trip."

He turned the car, revving the engine a bit more than necessary, but the lions didn't give a hoot.

"They must have been at it for a while," Francis said. "The first few days, they do it every five minutes, but by day five or six, they get tired."

They must have been at day seven.

"She must have a headache," Steve said.

Francis laughed and took off. Half a mile further, four lionesses slept piled over each other by the side of the road. They glanced at us passing, then went back to their slumber.

If they waited for the other two to be done, it looked like they'd have to wait for a while.

CHAPTER 34
ON CHEETAHS

WHO WOULD HAVE THOUGHT that the fastest animal on earth is a cat? In my previous cat encounters, most of them based on trading food for purrs and permission to pet, cats were way more likely to chill than to establish speed records. But this cat is not like the others.

The cheetah, the earth's fastest sprinter at 75 mph, was built for speed. She has a lean build, a small head, long legs, and a lengthy muscular tail that helps her balance and turn. She looks a bit like a leopard after an extended hunger strike.

Her streamlined body is well-suited for explosive bursts of speed, rapid acceleration, and sudden turns. She can cover 20 feet in a stride, more at top speed. When she runs, she spends most of the time flying with all four limbs in the air.

Similar to a Porsche 911 Turbo S, a cheetah can accelerate from 0 to 60 mph in less than three seconds. Her semi-retractable claws improve traction, and her stupendous tail helps her balance and acts as a rudder on sharp turns. Her long legs, large heart, and strong lungs are all designed for top speed. Her flexible spine works like a spring, extending and contracting to maximize stride length. The cheetah's only design problem is overheating, so she can't maintain top speed for too long.

Unlike other predators who hunt by smell, cheetahs hunt by sight, so they keep a lookout for prey from high vantage points. Their extraordinary field of vision — up to 210 degrees — lets them spot prey from miles away. To avoid low-light hunters like lions and leopards, cheetahs use the midday sun to their advantage, helped by the black "teardrop" markings that run from their eyes to their mouths to reduce glare.

They approach within 700 feet of the prey before starting the chase, which lasts less than a minute. In a couple of strides, they can slow down from 60 mph to follow the prey. After the last leap, they strangle their prey with a bite to the throat they maintain for a few minutes.

After the hunt, cheetahs need a few minutes to catch their breath and chill before eating while keeping an eye out for larger predators coming after their kill.

Their 40 percent success rate per hunt puts cheetahs ahead of lions (25 percent) and leopards (30 percent), but they lose a lot of kills to lions and hyenas. By the way, the spotted hyenas' success rate is about 70 percent, but they're not lonely hunters like the cheetahs.

Female cheetahs lead a solitary nomadic life in search of prey. They need a large range to feed themselves and their cubs, so they roam up to ten miles a day. They prefer open areas with bushes and trees to stalk their prey and avoid larger carnivores.

Males establish their territories in areas with rich prey and access to females. Sometimes a few males, usually siblings, will stick together to defend a valuable territory. They hunt together, groom each other by licking each other's faces and rubbing their cheeks, and share kills and visiting females.

Cheetahs are quite talkative: they purr when content, chirp

to call their cubs, and growl, meow, hiss, and yowl when they get upset.

At age two, females are ready for their first litter. But unlike lions and leopards, where females initiate the encounter, female cheetahs are shy. It's the male who approaches the female to declare his devotion by chirping, purring, or yelping before grabbing her nape to mate with her.

Three months later, the female gives birth to a litter of three or four vulnerable cubs that she hides in a den and moves often to keep safe. Sadly, she cannot defend them against lions or hyenas, so few cubs survive their first year. Their latest survival rate in the Serengeti was 17 percent.

The survivors open their eyes at one week and walk two weeks later. At two months, they trail mom and eat solid food. At four to six months, mom weans them and brings them live prey to teach them how to hunt, and they practice by pouncing, chasing, and wrestling each other.

At six months, they chase hares and young gazelles, but it will take them another six months to get their first kill. They leave the nest at around eighteen months when mom is ready for another litter.

Cheetahs need wide ranges to hunt, so habitat loss threatens them more than any of the other big cats. Humans hunt them to protect their livestock, the Maasai still use their skins in ceremonies, and wildlife traders steal their cubs to sell as pets.

There are so few cheetahs left that their reduced genetic variability makes them more vulnerable to diseases. No wonder they are classified as critically endangered from a conservation standpoint.

CHAPTER 35
HALFWAY DONE

We're officially past the first half of our 13-day safari, which is longer than most. Most people come for a week, but we're retired, so we have time, and we need more rest than the active youngsters who think nothing about zooming from park to park and changing beds every night. Like everything, it's a tradeoff.

We sat at lunch near a table of Americans who talked even more than they ate. Loud, too, so couldn't help but eavesdrop. Though, to be honest, this time I didn't enjoy it.

"When my daughter got her Ph.D....," a man said.

Another one interrupted.

"My son is a doctor, and he doesn't think much about Ph.Ds."

I left to get dessert, so I missed the rest, but that reminded me of another choice you'll have to make when booking your safari: Join a group, or go private?

Joining a group is less expensive. The flights, the eVisas, the park entries, the hotels, and the tips are the same. But dividing the cost of a safari vehicle and its guide-driver between six people instead of two certainly makes it more affordable.

If you are an extrovert, having companions to chat with is a bonus. You'll have new friends to share photos with, run things by, or ask for Tylenol when you run out.

But if you don't mind your own company and cherish silence, listening to the others' incessant chatter instead of the animals' calls, the birds' song or the savanna's silence may annoy you. So will wrestling for car seats, elbowing each other to take the best pictures, and waiting for latecomers to finish their coffee every morning. You'll also have little control over the schedule or the itinerary. But at least you won't have to put up with moochers hitching a ride, since the car will be full.

So, like everything else, it's a tradeoff. Choose wisely.

The trip to Lake Naivasha wasn't short, and it started poorly. I dragged my luggage to the car to find Francis looking gloomy.

"One of the resort managers had an emergency, and he needs a ride to the nearest town, a few hours away," Francis said. "It's your vehicle. You decide."

The man stood behind the car, looking healthy, content, and in no particular distress. But how could I say no?

"I bet that's how he always travels," Steve said.

I didn't take that bet, but I rearranged our stuff to make room for the guy and we got on our way. We were still in the park when we met a large herd of cows herded by three armed rangers. The horned suspects had failed their 6:30 curfew, and they were headed to jail.

"Where's the herder?" I asked Francis.

"He ran away."

"But won't he come back to get them?"

"Sure he will. After he gathers the money for the fine. Or the bribe."

Francis chatted to the rangers, like he always does; then we moved on. A few dozen potholes later, Tank stopped. An angry, muddy river blocked the road.

"Oooooh!" Francis said.

"Oooooh!" the resort manager agreed.

They stared thoughtfully at the river. Turning around to take an alternate road would cost us another couple of hours on top of the five we expected. But getting stuck in the river, or even worse, getting carried away, wouldn't exactly save time either.

We sat there thinking until Francis shook his head and turned around.

"The rangers should have told us," Steve said.

Francis agreed. Minutes later, we caught up with the cows, and Francis got chatting to the rangers again. Everyone talked and shrugged and shook their heads, then Francis U-turned again. That's a figure of speech, since the narrow road took some maneuvering, but we headed back to the river.

"The rangers said it's not too bad. The cows went through it, so we can too."

I don't know about that. The cows don't have iPhones and boots that take a week to dry and tight schedules. Well, they do have that.

Back we went, and stopped to stare at the rush of muddy water again, but this time two safari vehicles sat watching it thoughtfully from the other side.

We watched the water. They watched the water.

Then, out of nowhere, a mud-splattered truck coming behind us rushed forward at speed. He accelerated and skidded and swerved, splattering water like a broken fire hydrant.

"Ooooh! That's not good. Very bad," Francis said.

I couldn't help but agree.

"Very bad," Francis insisted, and that was the first time I heard him say anything negative about anyone. He always finds a nice angle, and when he can't find it, he shrugs.

But the truck made it to the other shore and took off, blasting mud behind him. The two safari vehicles on the other side crossed, slowly and carefully. The water reached almost to the windows, but they made it. We applauded. The drivers smiled, but the passengers behind them were green with fright.

Our turn. I wondered if my affairs were in order and my last will up to date as Francis took us slowly and safely to the other side, and off we went.

We stopped at one of the thousand curio shops lining the way. Like all the others, they advertised clean toilets and outstanding homemade merchandise. But this one had something others didn't: it was owned by Francis's friend, a Camba tribesman like him.

The man allowed me to use the bathroom before handing me the obligatory basket for my shopping. Since he was Francis's friend, I felt obliged to buy something. It shouldn't have been hard, since he had a hangar full of stuff. There were wood, stone, and bone carvings, from the size of a shot glass to full-sized giraffes. Colorful oil paintings of elephants, Maasai, and acacias. Weapons, blankets, and shields, and more beaded necklaces and bracelets than a giraffe had room to wear. The one thing he didn't have was a price.

I ignored his incessant chatter pointing me to this, that, or the other, as if I didn't own a pair of eyes on my own. I ignored the life-sized giraffes, the masks from his ancestors, and the pointed Maasai lances that would have been a hoot on the plane. I chose a palm-sized wood-carved mask and a stone hippopotamus no bigger than my thumb.

"That's it?" He didn't sound pleased.

"That's it," I confirmed. "We have a tiny house."

"But I can ship," he said.

"I bet."

"And I take credit cards."

I nodded.

Clearly disappointed, he headed to the desk and examined

my items like he'd never seen them before. He turned them upside down, then downside up. With a sorrowful sigh, he picked a piece of paper and a pencil and proceeded to instruct me into the Kenyan commerce habits.

"I write down the price."

He wrote down 8000 shillings. That's more than the price of a fat sheep or a goat. I don't know about you, but I'd rather have a live goat than a stone rhino.

I laughed and headed to the door.

"No, no," he said. "If this is no good for you, you write down what you wish to pay."

I calculated quickly. At TJ Maxx, I could probably get them both for ten dollars, five if they were on sale. I'd also get some points, and I wouldn't have to carry them all the way home. But he was Francis's friend. And I had used his toilet.

I wrote down 1500 Shillings. $10.

"This is my best and last price," I said. That's what they say in Thailand when they're done bargaining, and everyone knows it. Insisting past that is rude.

His face more pained than if someone stole his best cow, he wrote down 6000 Shillings.

I shook my head and headed to the door.

"That's not how we do business," he said, annoyed by my lack of cooperation. "Now you write down your next price."

"But this is how I do business. You do business your way, I do business my way. This is my last offer."

"How about 5000?" he asked. He was so shaken he forgot to write it down.

I shook my head.

"But you're my first customer of the day. If we don't make a deal, I won't sell anything the whole day! 2000?"

That's a heartbreaker. But for whom?

I shook my head.

"No. But don't worry, I'm sure someone else will stop by soon," I said.

He sighed as if I'd ripped out his heart.

"OK."

He wrapped the two tiny objects into a wrinkled brown paper and closed them with tape, then handed me the package that fit in my pocket. I handed him 2000 shillings and waited for the change.

He sighed.

"I'll get the change."

He disappeared. I waited and waited, under the judgmental eyes of the wooden giraffes, zebras, and warthogs, until I couldn't wait anymore. I walked out to find him chatting with Francis in the yard. No change seemed to be involved.

I waited some more. Steve came from wherever he'd been, carrying a cute tabby kitten.

"What are we waiting for?"

"The change," I said.

He played with the kitten, then set it down. The kitten started scratching.

"I hope you didn't get fleas," I said.

"He doesn't have them. I checked."

That was funny. Steve can't find the milk in the fridge door on a good day, and he'd find fleas on a kitten? I waited some more, then went to the man.

"My change?" I asked.

"It's coming."

So is Christmas, I thought, and considered handing back the items and asking for my money back when a young man came from somewhere down the road and handed him something. With the pained face of someone burying his only remaining parent, he handed me a wrinkled and very sweaty 500-shilling bill. I put it in my wallet, and we took off.

We stopped in Narok, a large and very busy town in the Maasai land to drop off the store manager for his emergency that didn't appear emergent at all, and tried to get a cable for the camera — Steve will tell you all about it later — before continuing to Lake Naivasha, our home for the day.

CHAPTER 36
LAKE NAIVASHA

The Naivasha Sopa Lodge is spectacular. It's a massive resort with splendid landscaped gardens where waterbucks and monkeys roam alongside tourists. It has beautiful African styling, wide lounges with wood fireplaces, and a splendid view over the lake. It also has numerous posters informing you that the management is not responsible for any injury or theft occurring on the premises, and staff that could use some training.

As soon as Tank stopped, a couple of uniformed men grabbed our heavy bags, and we ambled in loaded with all the odds and ends scattered through the car. I carried the computer case with our passports and money, my raincoat, my pillow, and my backpack. A smiling gentleman welcomed me and directed me to a gracious lady who offered me a lollipop and a mango juice I couldn't refuse. I stuck the pillow under one arm and the raincoat under the other, then took the lollipop in one hand and the mango juice in the other, and then, more loaded than the average mule, I followed the welcoming gentleman towards the baby grand piano in the lounge. I really hoped he wouldn't ask me to play, since not only do I suck at it, but I had run out of hands. Fortunately, he pointed us to sit in two leather armchairs, ordered us to relax, and demanded our passports.

I drank the juice, handed the lollipop to Steve, dropped the backpack, the pillow, and the raincoat on the floor, and started rummaging through my computer case for the passports. He took them and vanished, and I dropped into my seat.

Minutes later, he was back, demanding to know where Francis was. We shrugged. The man left again.

He took his sweet time until he eventually returned with our passports, a key, and a printed piece of paper.

"Your email here, your name here, and the signature here," he said, handing me a pen

I wrote my email, and my name. Then, since I'm not in the habit of signing things I didn't read, I started reading the paper. It was a page-full disclaimer stating that I indemnified the hotel, the managers, the porters, the waiters, the waterbucks, the monkeys, and anyone else passing by from any responsibility for whatever happened to me while I was there. Whichever of my belongings got stolen or destroyed, or in whichever manner I got injured, maimed or killed, I wouldn't hold them responsible or sue them, no matter what.

"Like seriously? If your cook poisons me, the cleaning staff stabs me in the back, or the roof collapses and kills me tonight, I promise to not sue you?" I asked, optimistic as ever. My heart raced and my blood pumped in my ears, but I kept my voice soft. I really hate it when people treat me like I'm stupid.

His smile melted.

"This is not what it says," he said.

"No? Did you read it?" I said.

"Everything is safe here," he said.

"I know, otherwise we wouldn't be here. So you have nothing to worry about. Since nothing will happen to us, we won't hold you liable."

The smile on his face would have soured milk.

"But this is a really safe place."

I nodded.

"I understand. I will not sign this." I handed back the sheet of paper, ready to grab my luggage and go. Where? No idea.

He took it.

"The gentleman there will help you with your luggage." He pointed to a gentleman by the door who was watching our encounter with the same entranced expression as the other fifty people in the room, and he made himself scarce without briefing us on the meal schedule, power outages, or anything else.

My heart pounding, my vision gray with anger, I headed to the luggage gentleman.

"Room number?" he asked.

"81."

"81?" He sounded so surprised I wondered if they had less than eighty rooms, and we'd been assigned to sleep in the shed.

We followed the luggage gentleman down the long, winding road to our quarters. The lodgings, four to each building, started with number one, so we had plenty of time to admire the landscaping, the clever Vervet monkeys rushing out of someone's room with some bars of soap, an elegant black-and white colobus monkey showing off her white fringed cape, and a couple of placid water bucks dutifully mowing the grass. By the time we got to 81, half a mile down the way, I was exhausted but chilled.

"Call for a cart if you want to come back," the porter ominously said after introducing us to our luxurious new quarters comprising two queen beds with mosquito nets, a living room with a view of the gardens and our first TV on this trip. The electricity worked, the water was hot, and we even had Wi-

Fi. It hadn't been easy, but we'd gotten to the best room of our trip.

We enjoyed it for all of ten minutes before heading back for lunch and our scheduled boat ride. The lunch — buffet style — was delicious, and our loyal Tank waited with Francis in the parking lot.

We got stopped twice at the two guarded gates before heading down the potholed street to look for the boat place for our included boat tour. It turned out to be an unimpressive grassy field guarded by a hand-operated barrier and patrolled by three friendly bulldogs.

The lady in charge, an attractive young woman with a dazzling smile, kitted us in brand-new orange flotation devices and made sure we'd tied them right.

"The boat trip around the lake takes an hour. If you want to walk around the island with a guide to see the animals and stretch your legs, that's another half an hour and 25 dollars per person."

Steve sighed.

"It's gonna rain."

"So what? Can't you stretch your legs and look at animals in the rain?"

He glared at me.

"What for? Haven't you seen plenty of animals already?"

"But not on foot. And never close enough to touch them."

He shrugged.

"We don't have the money anyhow. I left it in the safe."

"How much do you have?"

"Twenty-five dollars. That's it."

I counted mine. I had another fifteen in fives, plus a couple of ones I kept for tips.

I turned to the lady.

"We have forty altogether. Maybe we could have a shorter trip? Like only 25 minutes?"

She seemed persuadable, so I pulled out the money. In my experience, people are much easier to convince when they actually see the money than when it's all just talk.

"Oops," I said. "I lied. I have four fives. $45 total."

She smiled wider and absconded the money like a magician. Steve sighed.

The gentleman who had opened the gate, a tall man who had yet to say a word, nodded towards the boat. We headed that way, but it wasn't close. Two minutes later, Steve got antsy.

"What the heck? We're going to take the walk right here?" he growled.

Apparently not. The man held the boat for us and started the engine. We watched the shore slip away and headed towards the island, looking for the animals we'd been promised.

"Hippopotamus," the boatman said, pointing to a hippo mother with her baby, and filling me with amazement. Not about the hippos, but the man. He hadn't said a word throughout our encounter, so I thought he spoke no English. I was mistaken.

He took us to the island the long way, showing us a multitude of birds, plants, and plenty more hippos. Once there, we parked near three other boats to watch a substantial herd of water buffaloes darkening the ground by the landing, and waited. And waited.

"What are we waiting for?" I finally asked.

"For the water buffaloes to cross. We don't want to be anywhere near them, because they can be dangerous."

It looked like we'd be waiting a long time. The water buffaloes took their sweet time grazing the spare grass by the shore. They stood there, thoughtful, like a herd of philosophers hanging their massive black heads. What are they thinking about? I wondered. The upcoming elections? Climate change? Dinner?

They eventually moved on. Stiff from sitting and about as graceful as two rhinos, we got off the boat thanks to a young man who introduced himself as Joseph. He grabbed us before we fell in the mud, thus preventing us from seeing Lake Naivasha from inside, took us ashore and led us to the animals.

Lake Naivasha is a sweet water lake at over 6000 feet altitude, the highest elevation of the Great Rift Valley. Its crescent-shaped island, aptly named Crescent Island, is a wildlife sanctuary populated by a good number of herbivores but completely devoid of predators. That's why you may walk here, unlike in any other park we've been. Crescent Island is not a national park, it's a private conservancy, but it's still subject to the Kenyan National Wildlife Services regulations.

As soon as we left the tricky path through the mud for solid ground, we met a bunch of wildebeest. Wildebeest are not rare, since they make up the vast majority of the Great Migration, but these were the first ones we had met, and we stopped to wonder at their astonishing mismatched features.

"We say that God made them from whatever he had left over after he finished building all the other animals. They have the horns of a buffalo, the tail of a horse, the stripes of a zebra, the mane of a lion, and the beard of a goat," Joseph said.

He was right. They also have the hump of a camel, only darker. Unfortunately, God must have run short of brains, so he didn't give them much. They say the zebras migrate with the wildebeest to avoid getting eaten, since the poor beasts don't have enough sense to run away from danger. They'll stand and watch Mara's crocodiles drag their friends under the water, wondering what happened, instead of taking off to safety. Fortunately, this island is safe even for them.

Wildebeest, a.k.a. gnu, are large antelopes, and they are

much sought after, despite their ragtag looks. Lions, leopards, and hyenas love having them for dinner. So do humans. Biltong, their dried meat, is an African delicacy. Their hide makes excellent leather, and their tails are turned into fly-whisks and fans.

Wildebeest also fertilize the soil and represent a major tourist attraction, but they compete with cattle for grazing and can transmit diseases. They also spread ticks, lungworms, tapeworms, and flies.

We passed some handsome waterbucks, with sculpted spiral horns and shiny fur, then continued to the zebras, where we found a lovely surprise: a fluffy one-week-old baby zebra who was too young to be afraid of us. He stopped his grazing to stare like we were something special instead of following his mom and older brother, who had moved away.

"His brown stripes will darken with age. As he rolls in the grass and the mud, his furry coat will disappear and his skin will become sleek and shiny, like his mom's."

Next to the zebras, a tall giraffe with two babies stretched her neck to show her young ones how to pick an acacia's tiny green leaves with their lips and black tongue without touching the 2-inch thorns.

"Zebras and giraffes like to hang out together. Since they're so tall, giraffes spot predators from afar and call the alarm, and their kick is strong enough to break a lion's jaw. Zebras kick too," Joseph said.

"This one is a Rothschild giraffe. See the pattern of her coat, like leaves? That one's her baby. He's seven months old. The other one is an orphan. His mom broke her leg, and the vet had to put her down, because broken legs don't heal in giraffes. Fortunately, this one adopted him and now takes care of them both. They already graze, but they still need milk until they're about one."

We wondered at the baby giraffes, which, at just seven months, were way taller than Steve, who's so much older. They ambled awkwardly on their oddly shaped legs to munch on branches so spiny that I wouldn't dare touch, but kept their eyes on us while flicking their ears and swishing their tails to get rid of flies.

Sadly, our time was over, and Joseph took us back to the boat. Steve slipped him a well-deserved tip, and we got back on the lake.

We watched the shiny black cormorants dry their wings in the sun after swimming underwater to fish, and listened to the hippos snort, fart, and call each other nasty names. We basked in the sun and watched the African fish eagles dive after the tiny fish our guide threw them from the boat. With their dark bodies, white heads, and curved yellow beaks, they're so much like the bald eagles it's uncanny.

It was a fun trip and worth the money, even more so when our boatman, whose name I never knew, started talking.

He was from Nakuru, fifty miles away, and went to college to train as a guide. A few years ago, he found this job and moved here. His parents still live in Nakuru, but now he has a family of his own.

"Kids?" I asked.

"Four. Two boys and two girls."

"How old?"

"The oldest is eight."

"Wow. Your wife must be a busy lady."

"She is. But it's easier now that three of them go to school."

"Is school free in Kenya?"

"Somewhat."

"How so?"

"We still have to pay for activities, sports, books, and uniforms. Even for the brooms and the duster."

"So what's free, then?"

He laughed.

"The teachers, I guess."

"And lunch?"

"No. We buy their lunch."

"Do they learn languages in school?"

"Yes. starting in fourth grade."

"What languages?"

"French. Chinese, Spanish. They can choose."

"Not English?"

"Yes. And Swahili. But that's a given. The classes are in English."

"Not Swahili?"

"That's just a language class. But math, geography, and everything else is taught in English."

That explains why everyone here speaks excellent English, albeit with a slightly different accent. From business managers to doormen and people running after Tank to sell us mangoes in the street, they're all as fluent in English as I am.

He took us back to Francis, who'd been chilling with the attractive young lady for the time we'd been gone, and before long, we were back in our room.

Since we had internet, we booked our return flights from Bangkok to our Thai home. We're nearing the end of our journey, and it's time to get ready.

By the time we were done, we were too tired to take the long hike to the dining room, so I made tea and sliced the Madeira cake I'd bought at a market for less than a dollar. It looked like a pound cake and it was just as unspectacular, but it soothed our growling stomachs enough to let us sleep.

CHAPTER 37
ON ZEBRAS

Thanks to their unique black-and-white striped outfits, zebras are some of the most easily recognizable animals on the planet. Still, nobody knows for sure what the stripes are for, other than allowing researchers to tell them apart.

The oldest hypothesis suggests that a zebra's stripes allow her to blend better into her environment so she's harder to spot by predators. But after seeing a few thousand zebras, I can assure you that they do not blend in the savanna. Whoever thought they did needs glasses.

The confusion hypothesis posits that stripes confuse predators by making it harder to distinguish the individuals from the group or count them. That left me confused. From what I saw, neither lions nor hyenas seemed particularly picky about who exactly they ate, nor did they appear prone to complicated mathematical exploits like counting zebras.

The fly protection hypothesis pushes things even further. It states that disease-spreading horseflies get confused by the stripes and can't decide whether the white or the black stripe looks tastier, so they forgo biting them altogether. I agree that making choices is hard, considering the extended time I spend to pick my lunch at the buffet, but that difficulty didn't make me lose any weight. Just the opposite. When I can't make up my mind, I just eat everything. But maybe horseflies are pickier.

The thermoregulatory hypothesis proposes that the stripes help control the zebra's temperature by creating convection air currents that converge, resulting in cooling air swirls. Still, no research has proven that zebras are cooler (temperature wise) than any other herbivore in the savanna, even though they do look cool.

Finally, the social function hypothesis states that stripes help individuals recognize each other and bond. In 1871, Charles Darwin wrote that "a female zebra would not admit the addresses of a male ass until he was painted to resemble a zebra." One can only wish that his observation proved true across species. But enough about stripes. Let's move on.

Zebras are so closely related to horses and mules that they can mate, giving birth to zebroids. A cross between a zebra and a horse is called a zorse, one between a zebra and a donkey is a zonkey, and a zoni is the cross of a zebra with a pony. Zebroids are often born sterile.

But, unlike horses and mules, zebras have never really been domesticated, possibly because of their lousy attitude and unpredictable temper. Zebras can be hostile and aggressive. Furthermore, they have a ducking reflex which makes them almost impossible to lasso. And, unlike wild horses, they have no clear family structure or hierarchy.

Zebras prefer grass, but they'll also eat bark, leaves, fruits, and roots. That's why they look well fed even during draughts. They mingle with giraffes and wildebeest to graze, in a doubly strategic move. Since they tower above the savanna, the giraffes will call the alarm when danger arises. And, since they are more agile and strategic than their wildebeest neighbors, zebras are more likely to escape when chased by a hungry lion. As the joke goes, if you and your friend get chased by a hungry bear, don't worry about running faster than the bear. You only need to run faster than your friend.

Currently, there are three species of zebras left: the plains zebra, the mountain zebra, and the Grévy's zebras. They look similar, but they differ in size and the style of their stripes, with the Grévy's zebras being substantially bigger and sporting narrower stripes.

Zebras also differ in their social and mating behaviors. Plains and mountain zebra mares will only mate with one stallion, since they live in lifelong stable families comprising a stallion, several mares, and their foals.

Unlike them, Grévy's zebras live in loosely associated herds, so their mating is promiscuous, with multiple males vying for the mares' affections. To adapt to that challenging situation, Grévy's zebras developed larger testes (i.e., grew bigger balls) that make them more successful in sperm competition.

Zebras, like horses, bond through social grooming. Friends sniff each other, rub their cheeks, then move along each other's bodies to sniff one another's business parts. They may also rub their shoulders and lay their heads on one another. To groom one another, they nibble and rake their teeth along each other's neck and back. They snort and gasp when startled, and squeal when in pain. To threaten another, they flatten their ears, bare their teeth and whip their tails.

Zebras can survive up to a week without water, but they will drink every day when given a chance, binging on more than four gallons a day. Zebras sleep standing during the day but lie down at night. To scratch, they rub against trees and roll, just like horses, and they enlist our old friends, the oxpeckers, to rid them of ticks and parasites.

After a gestation of a year, the zebra gives birth to a foal who is initially striped in brown and white. He can run within an hour, but, like ducks, he's pre-programmed to imprint on anything that moves, so his mother needs to keep him away from the others until he learns to recognize her by her stripes, her smell, and her voice. He grazes in a few days but will continue to nurse for a year.

Zebras are very protective of their young. When babies are threatened, the whole herd surrounds them, forming a circle that defends them by kicking and biting the intruder. The stallion will charge at any predator coming close to protect the foal. If a mother dies, an auntie will usually adopt her foal and bring him up like her own.

Foals mature around age four, when young stallions start to fight, bite and kick, to build their own family. They try to recruit mares from their birth harem, but the old stallion will fight to keep them as long as he is fit. Old, unhealthy stallions will eventually have their harems taken over.

Zebras classify as endangered from a conservation standpoint, mainly because of habitat fragmentation. They are also hunted for their hide and meat. Even today, zebra skins will sell for over $1,000.

CHAPTER 38
AMBOSELI

The trip to Amboseli was the longest one yet. We left Lake Naivasha after a sumptuous breakfast — pastries, yogurt, cereal, eggs made to order, bacon, sausage of two kinds, grilled tomatoes, baked beans, and a few other dishes I couldn't recognize, plus coffee and tea brought to the table. I ate so much I had to drag myself to Tank, who was waiting with Francis at the door, but I was sure the potholes would settle everything soon. They sure did. Before long, I had to ask Francis about a toilet.

Unlike America and most of Europe, Kenya does not appear to have rest stops. So, we stopped at a gas station, where a smiling young man handed me a set of keys and directed me behind the building.

Four adjacent concrete cells stood at the back of the yard, two doorless and two with locked doors. The open ones had a hole in the ground that made them into a latrine. The locked ones also had a hole in the ground but were far less clean. I thus figured that the no-door were the male urinals, whereas the others were for ladies and heavier affairs that involved squatting.

I did my best to hold my breath, but the outside air afterwards felt good. I returned the key with a tip and got back in the car, and that's when I realized something: the reason we had stopped at all those shops featuring toilets was not only so Francis can get his commission. We stopped there because they offered the only Western-style toilets available. Most gas stations don't bother to build and maintain something that most of their customers don't require, so it came to the curio shops to satisfy this market niche, and thus attract clients. It makes perfect sense. I just wish I could just pay for the privilege, or that haggling for trinkets wouldn't be such a hassle. But it is what it is, and if I didn't like it, I should have stayed home.

We skirted Nairobi and caught a glimpse of Kibera, Africa's largest slum, home to more than a million people. We stared at the sea of jumbled houses made of corrugated metal and wondered how people live here. No power or running water, I bet. But do they even have an address? Does the mailman bring their mail? How can somebody even find them if they visit? And how about kid's schools?

I researched it later. A 2009 survey found that the average Kibera resident earns less than US$2 per day, and 12 percent of them live with HIV. Assault and rape are common, and most children don't go to school. Most residents have no electricity, running water, or medical care, and poor hygiene causes a lot of health problems.

The government tried to replace the slum with high-rise apartments and relocate the residents to them after completion, but it failed.

"Isn't this a political issue?" I asked Francis. "These people vote, don't they?"

"It is. They tried to convince them to let them build real houses for them, but they refused."

"Why?"

"Because they now own the land. If the government builds on it, they won't own it anymore."

I pondered on how hard change is, even if it's for the good, as we continued on a short highway with tolls, then took another country road with goats parked all over the gas station, informal markets doing hot business, and daring vendors that chased Tank to sell us stuff: Green plums, potato chips, water bottles, and something looking like orange fishnet stockings.

"What are those?" I asked Francis.

"To wash with. That's what you rub your back with."

Like a loofah, I figured, but I couldn't understand how people can make a living selling that to passing cars. But, if nothing else, they kept fit, chasing Tank while trying to throw their stuff in through the windows. No wonder they're the best runners in the world, I thought, while I get winded tying my boots. No matter where you go around here, you're above 6,000 feet, so the air is thin and breathing requires work.

We drove on, up and up, behind smoky trucks we couldn't pass on the hairpin curves, avoiding the tight spots, the goats crossing the road and the rows of scooters carrying towers of egg crates, bags of coal, bundles of firewood, and up to three live sheep each, until we got to the top. At the viewpoint, we were graced with a view of the Great Rift Valley, a reasonable toilet inside a curio shop populated by wooden elephants, spotted giraffes, and a mob of haggard tourists waving their credit cards.

I took the picture of a lovely young couple, then they took ours.

"There's something magic about smiling," I said. "It demands a response. Did you notice how they started smiling as soon as they looked at us through the camera?"

Steve, who's not much of a smiler, gave me a side glance.

"I thought it was because I'd forgotten to zip my fly."

As we got close to Amboseli, the cows multiplied, the men became taller and thinner, and they all carried — you guessed it — sticks.

"We're back in Maasai territory," Francis said. "Amboseli is also Maasai, but it's a national park, not a national reserve, like Maasai Mara."

I didn't quite catch the difference, other than here they didn't bring in cows at night, but that got us talking about the Maasai. Unlike most Kenyans, who are Christians of various denominations and therefore only have one wife at a time, the Maasai are polygamous.

"How many wives do they have?"

"As many as they can afford. They have to pay for them in cows."

"Does the girl have a say in all this?"

"No. The wife talks to the parents, and if they agree, it's a deal."

"The wife?"

"The first wife. The first wife chooses the second, the second chooses the third, and so on."

I was befuddled.

"So the wife chooses the next wife, not the man?"

"Right."

"But why?"

"When a man is old enough to marry, his parents find him a wife. They agree with her parents and get him married. Then, maybe a year later, when he's ready for another wife, he tells his wife: 'I want to marry again.' So she looks around the village for a girl she can get along with. Because some girls are big-headed and don't listen. If she likes the girl, she speaks to her parents and if they agree, she tells the husband: 'I got you a wife.' The new wife comes to the home, but she has no contact with the husband until the first wife trains her. She teaches her what he likes and how he wants things done."

"You mean as in sex or housework?"

"Everything. Then, when she's ready, he'll make a sound like this," Francis grunted. "Then she knows he's ready to have sex with her. When he's done, he makes that noise again, and she knows it's time to leave. They don't talk to each other or touch or anything. They don't even look at each other. Then, when it's time, the second wife chooses the third wife. That's because they have to get along so they can work together. Women build the houses they live in, which are made of mud and cow dung. They also cook, bring water, build fires, and do everything that needs doing. The men do nothing but look after the cows. Before, they used to hunt, but they no longer do. So the women do all the work."

Being a Maasai wife sounded terrible, but being a Maasai man was totally incomprehensible to me.

"But what's the point of having all these wives if he doesn't even get to choose them?"

"That's how they live. This isn't about love. It's about having children. The more children they have, the richer they are and have higher status."

I tried to wrap my head around this concept, but I failed.

"But what happens to the other Maasai men? The ones who have no wives?"

Francis looked at me like I was nuts.

"They all have wives."

"But if there are, say, a hundred men in the village, and a hundred women. Say that thirty men have three wives each. That means that a lot of men will be left with no wives."

"They'll go find women in another village."

I tried and tried, but I couldn't explain to him that the math didn't work.

Francis continued his Maasai life story.

"Say a man's cousin from another village comes to visit. The man will give him one of his wives for while he's there. He'll tell her: So-and-so, you take care of my cousin, and she knows what that means."

"You mean he'll lend her to him?"

"Yes."

"What happens if she gets pregnant with the cousin?"

"Nothing happens. The child stays in the family."

I was so flabbergasted I couldn't speak, but Francis was still thinking about that math.

"And women are more. They live longer. The men die sooner, because of the stress."

"The stress?! What stress?"

"When a man has a problem, he doesn't tell anyone. He keeps it inside, and it grows and grows until it kills him. If a woman has a problem, she goes and tells a friend, and it's all gone. That's why they live longer."

This was when Steve intervened.

"It's the stress of all those damn wives. That's what kills them," he said.

I gave him the "we'll talk later" look and turned to Francis.

"What happens with the wives when the men die? Do they remarry?"

"They go to his brothers or his cousins. They stay in the family."

"What if the cousins and the brothers don't want them?"

"The elders gather and say: So-and-so, you take this one. And so-and-so, you take this one. And they know what they mean. So the wives and the children stay in the family."

The idea of these women having absolutely no say in what happened to them was unfathomable to me.

"Do the girls go to school?"

"Yes. The girls and the boys."

"How long?"

"Until they're eighteen and grown up. By law, they can't marry until they're 18; otherwise, their parents and their husband go to jail."

There's that, at least.

"How about female genital mutilation? Does that happen?"

"It's against the law."

"But does it happen?"

"Of course."

That got me soured on the Maasai, no matter how brave and good looking they are, with their manly sticks and red blankets. Francis felt my discomfort.

"But it's not the same in other tribes," he said.

"Tell me about it."

But first, let's see the Maasai's point of view.

CHAPTER 39
THE MAASAI IN THEIR OWN WORDS

"THE MAASAI PEOPLE *of East Africa live in southern Kenya and northern Tanzania along the Great Rift Valley on semi-arid and arid lands. The Maasai occupy a total land area of 160,000 square kilometers with a population of approximately half a million people, but since many Maasai see the census as government meddling, they will miscount their numbers.*

"A majority of the Maasai population lives in Kenya. They live in kraals arranged in a circle with a fence made of acacia thorns to prevent lions from attacking the cattle. The men fence the kraal, while women build the houses. Traditionally, kraals are shared by an extended family.

"The Inkajijik (Maasai houses) are loaf-shaped and made of mud, sticks, grass, cow dung, and cow urine. Women build the houses, bring water, collect firewood, milk the cattle, and cook. Warriors provide security while boys herd the livestock. The elders direct day-to-day activities. Every morning before livestock leave to graze, the head elder sits on his chair and announces the schedule everyone will follow.

"The Maasai are a semi-nomadic people who lived under a communal land management system that allows sustainably

using resources. Each section manages its own territory. Normally, reserve pastures are fallow, but if the draught is harsh, sections boundaries are ignored and people graze animals throughout the land until the rainy season. According to Maasai, no one should be denied access to water and land.

"Cattle, goats, and sheep are the Maasai's primary source of income. Livestock is traded for other livestock, cash, or products such as milk and siege. Families establish close ties through exchanging cattle. 'May the Creator give us cattle and children,' says a Maasai prayer. Cattle and children are the most valuable aspects of the Maasai people's lives.

"The Maasai economy depends increasingly on the market economy. Livestock products are sold to other groups for beads, clothing, and grains. Cows and goats are sold for uniforms and school fees for children. These days, young Maasai men and women will go to markets and sell, not just goats and cows, but also beads, cellphones, charcoal, and grain.

"This entrepreneurial spirit is new in our society. Because of the Group Ranch project, we became more entrenched in a market economy and, hence, more impoverished.

"Traditionally, the Maasai rely on cow meat, milk, and blood for their protein and caloric needs. People drink blood on special occasions. It is given to circumcised persons, women who gave birth, and the sick. Also, drunk elders use the blood to ease hangovers. Blood is protein rich and good for the immune system, but its use in the traditional diet is waning because of the reduction of livestock numbers.

"More recently, the Maasai have grown dependent on food produced in other areas such as maize, rice, potatoes, and cabbage. Some Maasai who live near crop farmers engage in land cultivation as their primary mode of subsistence because plot sizes are not large enough to accommodate herds of animals. Our people frown upon this. Maasai believe that using

the land for crop farming is a crime against nature. Once you cultivate the land, it is no longer suitable for grazing.

"Private ownership was, until recently, a foreign concept to the Maasai, but a program of commercializing livestock and land was forced on us. Our land was subdivided into ranches. Some Maasai people subdivided their individual ranches into small plots, sold to private developers.

"The new land management system polarized our people; some Maasais have increased their wealth at others' expense. The largest land loss, however, has been to national parks and reserves, where the Maasai are restricted from accessing critical water sources, pastures, and salt licks. Subdividing Maasai land reduced land size for cattle herding, reduced the number of cows per household, and reduced food production. As a result, the Maasai society, once proud and self-sufficient, now faces many challenges. The poverty among the Maasai people is inconceivable. It is sad to see a society with a long tradition of pride being a beggar for relief food because of imposed foreign concepts of development.

"The future of the Maasai is uncertain. One thing is certain: the Maasai culture is quickly eroding at the expense of civilization.

"Facts about lion hunting:

"Imagine having a lion three meters away from you! Hunting a lion with a spear and shield is an experience of a lifetime.

"Although lion hunting was an activity of the past, lions are occasionally hunted when they attack Maasai livestock. Cattle are central to Maasai livelihood.

"Imagine losing your bank account to a scammer? Losing cattle to lions is a tragedy for a Maasai family. Maasai income comes solely from the cows. Therefore, protecting the cows from

lions has always been a matter of grave concern for every Maasai.

"With compensation for cattle killed by lions, the warriors have been leaving the lions alone. A share of revenue generated from game reserves in Maasai land could only improve the situation.

"Lions are not currently endangered but their life remains uncertain, not because of the warriors but because of rabies.

"The practice of lion hunting and other wildlife has been banned in East Africa. Unless, of course, if you are wealthy enough to join the Western Hunters Club who pay an enormous amount of money to hunt lions for trophy. Otherwise, lion hunting has been outlawed in East Africa."

Excerpted from: © Maasai Association, https://maasai-association.org/maasai.html

If the Maasai intrigue you, I recommend checking out the link above. There's a wealth of information on their ceremonies and other aspects of their lives, and there are opportunities to donate should you be so inclined.

CHAPTER 40
KENYAN MARRIAGES

WE'RE STILL on our long drive to Amboseli as Francis tells us the story of his marriage. As usual, Steve sits in front, where he can stretch his long legs and see better, and I sit in the back, where I have access to water, snacks, phone chargers, and even occasional naps. I distribute the cookies I acquired along the way, and we munch and listen.

"I was one of a big family. All kids from one mother. We lived in a village. When I grew up, I left home and went to Mombasa to study and work. I stayed with my older sister, who was married, and I worked as a taxi driver and as a street preacher. Everybody knew me."

"You mean you just went and preached in the streets?"

"Yes. Everyone called me Brother. People in Mombasa still do. But that was thirty years ago. We had no phones and no email. We wrote our letters by hand and looked for someone who was going home to take our letter there, then waited for someone to bring back the answer. It took weeks. One day I got a letter from my parents, who wanted me to come home."

"Why?"

"We got you married," they said. "Your wife is already home with us. You need to come back and be with her."

"They got you married when you weren't even there?"

"Yes."

"And?"

"I wrote back to ask who my wife was. When they answered, I got so mad. I sent them a long, angry letter and told them to get rid of her; otherwise, I wasn't coming home."

"Why? You knew her and didn't like her?"

"Yes. She was the daughter of my mother's brother."

"Why didn't you like her?"

Francis shrugged. As always, when he has nothing good to say, he'd rather keep quiet.

"And then?"

"My sister went home and spoke to my parents. She told them to get rid of the lady. So they did. They sent her home, and I went home after that."

"Were they mad?"

"They never said a thing. Like it never happened. But I knew I had to find myself a girl; otherwise, they'd find one for me. So, my friends and I went into the village to look at girls. There was this little girl I used to know when I was a Sunday School teacher. She was small, and I always took care of her when others bullied her. I told her: You stay with me, and I'll take care of you. I'll marry you someday. But I was only kidding. She was so small."

"How old were you?"

"Ten, maybe?"

"And how old was she?"

"Two years younger."

"And then?"

"My friends said I should look up so-and so, but I laughed. She was just a little girl. So we went through the village to look at girls, and then I saw her. She was no longer small, and she was so pretty. My heart felt funny when I saw her."

"And then?"

"First, I talked to her, then I wrote to her when I went back to Mombasa. And she wrote back. When I came back home, I spoke to her parents."

"What did they say?"

"They said yes, even though I only gave them three goats."

"Why three goats?"

"That's the tradition. It's like an engagement ring. You give them three goats, and they slaughter one for the party. Then, for the marriage, you must give them cows."

"How many cows?"

"About thirty."

"Do they have to be big and fat, or is it good enough if they're skinny?"

"They don't have to be very big, but they must be healthy. And not too skinny. Otherwise, you don't look good."

"How much do cows cost?"

"Depends on the cow. A good one will be about thirty-five to fifty thousand shillings."

That's about $300. I realized that we'd changed enough money in the airport to buy a cow, though not a big one. I also realized that when you donate $1000 to some foundation to buy a heifer for a family in need, you're paying for way more than that cow.

"They also like sheep. You know sheep?"

"I know sheep, though not personally."

"They like sheep, especially if they're really fat, with a big rump. The women melt the fat and put it into bottles."

"They use it for their hair?"

"No, they use it to cook."

"So what happened to the cows you owed them?"

"I should have given them thirty cows. But I went and told them: There's no point in me giving you cows. When I marry your daughter, I will become your son. I will take care of you like I'll take care of my parents. That's better than giving you cows. Cows get sick and die, but I'll take care of you forever. So they said yes. But they would have said yes anyhow. They knew I was a hard-working boy, and I taught Sunday school and all."

"So, you married her?"

"Yes."

"What a beautiful story!"

"We've been married thirty-five years, and we have three children, two boys and a girl. The youngest one is 21. He's in college. The oldest two are married and have babies."

"You still love her?"

"I do. And there's a new love that comes to you when you have grandchildren. I never knew that, but it's like a sweetness in your heart. Whenever I hold them, my heart is full."

I was still pondering the complicated story of human relationships when we finally got to Kimba Camp Amboseli. We were tired and dusty, but we had a new understanding of Kenya's amazing variety. People here are not all the same, nor are their lives. Every tribe has their own customs and traditions, unlike everyone else's.

CHAPTER 41
KIMBA CAMP AMBOSELI

THE KIMBA CAMP IS RUSTIC. The central buildings, as always, contain the reception, a bar, a restaurant, and the never-missing curio shop. They also have the only internet. But the tents, as they call them, even though rustic, have a fan, drinking water, and even a small refrigerator — a luxury we haven't yet seen. The bed has mosquito nets, and there's even an extension cable big enough to charge our many devices. All in all, we were delighted with our new digs. We did a bit of urgent laundry and got ready for our first game drive, most eager to meet Mt. Kilimanjaro.

But I was a tad underwhelmed, to be honest. I expected something steep, jagged, and imposing, but the famous mountain looked like a salad bowl turned upside down. Sure it's snow-capped, and it has long dark grooves, but from down here it doesn't look like much of a mountain. Nothing like the stunning peaks of Everest and Annapurna. Still, I looked it up.

Kilimanjaro, Africa's highest mountain and the highest freestanding mountain in the world, sits at 19,341 feet above the sea. It's a dormant volcano with three cones: Kibo, Mawenzi, and Shira, all extinct but Kibo, which still smokes and might erupt again someday.

Kilimanjaro is the fourth of the Seven Summits (the tallest mountains on every continent) and very popular with climbers because the climb is less challenging than the Himalayas. Still, elevation and low temperatures can make Kilimanjaro a difficult trek. According to the Kilimanjaro Christian Medical Center, twenty-five people died climbing the mountain between 1996 and 2003: fourteen from altitude sickness, three from trauma, four from heart attacks, two from pneumonia, and one from appendicitis.

I had plenty of time to look up these facts, since our game drive in Amboseli turned into a birdwatching trip. Other than a few elephants, a busy tortoise heading to an undisclosed location, and a few gazelles swishing their tails, in our many hours of driving the potholed roads of Amboseli, we saw nothing but birds.

But let me start with the half-dozen Maasai ladies waiting by the park entrance to sell us stuff. More wooden giraffes, beaded necklaces, sculpted platters, and more bracelets than an octopus could wear. I closed the window and said no, avoiding eye contact, but I watched them from the corner of my eye. How do they live, these women who get sold for cows, lent to their husband's visiting cousin, and are tasked with procuring their husband's next wife? What do they think? How do they feel?

Their faces told me nothing. Tall and lean, wrapped in the ubiquitous red blankets, one around the shoulders and another one around the waist, they walked proudly under the merchandise weighing them down. Not only did they have their hands full, but they wore dozens of beaded necklaces around their necks, countless bracelets jingling on their wrists, and heavy earrings that dangled from their elongated earlobes to below their shoulders. They stood watching for the next crop of tourists with narrow eyes as sharp as those of hawks.

"Why do they have no hair?" I asked Francis, who, by the way, shaves his head too.

"Because here they think that bald is beautiful. They look prettier without hair."

I didn't know what to say to that. I suppose it shows the earrings better.

I watched the senior lady directing the others with no smile on her face. The first wife, I thought, wondering what life must be like when you never talk to your husband. How do you even argue? I wondered, as Francis drove us into Amboseli.

The whole place is a marsh — other than Lake Amboseli, which is only a part-time lake, since it runs dry every dry season, allowing safari vehicles to cross through it to the park's other side. That makes Amboseli a great place to visit during the dry season, when many other parks get dry and the animals turn to the marshes. But since this year it rained every day, sometimes all day, the animals didn't come.

That left Amboseli to the mud lovers — water buffaloes, elephants, and birds. Some we already knew, like the ostriches, looking like tall men in tuxedos who forgot their trousers, with their dark feathery bodies and naked legs; the pelicans with yellow tote bags hanging under powerful beaks and shrewd eyes always watching for some handout; the crowned cranes, their graceful feathered heads looking out of synch with their bodies. They look stark black-and-white in flight, but they burst with color on the ground, with their gray feathery collar, brown tail, orange wingtips, and crimson face. To crown it all, the fluffy golden feathers on their heads flutter in the breeze, making them look like overdressed starlets at the Oscars.

We stopped to watch a couple of them feed five fluffy chicks.

The tiny chicks stumbled through the grass while their elegant parents strutted around on their skinny legs that bend backwards, scratching the ground in search of breakfast. Whenever they found a bug or a worm, they served it to the chicks who were waiting with their beaks open wide. It was breakfast and a lesson rolled into one, plus an impressive cooperation. No questions were asked, no directions were given, but the chicks got fed one by one like they were on a conveyor belt, and I heard no complaints.

Further down, a long row of flamingoes walked shoulder to shoulder through the shallow water, fishing as they went. Their long feet stirred the mud, prompting breakfast towards the shore. They stepped forward as one, just as coordinated as the Rockettes and way more elegant. These were greater flamingoes, classy and 5 feet tall, with blushing pink feathers, not the smaller, flashier, lesser flamingoes.

We watched a couple of small black crakes with yellow beaks and bright red eyes amble on stick-like red legs searching for food amongst the white and purple waterlilies.

"The hippos should be close. These birds like to sit on their backs and eat their bugs," Francis said. Not today. The hippos, like everyone else, were MIA.

A flock of blacksmith plovers standing in the road cursed at us when they had to fly away. They're easy to recognize by their sharp black-and-white pattern and their tink-tink-tink metallic sounds.

"It sounds just like a blacksmith," Francis said. That got me thinking. To me it sounded like a fork scratching a cheese grater, but what do I know about birds? Or blacksmiths, for that matter? Further down, a couple of them were harassing a crowned crane five times their size, coming at her from every angle as she strutted on her tall legs looking for food.

"They're protecting their nest," Francis said. "They like to lay their eggs on the ground by the road, and she'll eat them if she finds them."

Silly birds. If I knew how to lay eggs, I swear I'd find them a better place than the side of the road, especially with all these miles of marshes around. I guess they don't call it birdbrain for nothing. But at least they were determined. Before long, the crane had had enough and took off for greener pastures, leaving the blacksmiths to their family building.

We stopped for lunch by a tall hill offering 360-degree views of the marshes. We fought the wind stealing our napkins and ate our vegetable sandwiches and boiled eggs, watched with utter fascination by some tiny gray sparrows and some metallic blue birds with shrewd round eyes who had learned that it's easier to beg than look for food. That reminded us how important it is to stay out of animals' lives and let nature takes its course. On the way down, we read the informative panels about the park and its inhabitants and learned that:

1. Kilimanjaro quenches the thirst of millions of people and wildlife in this vast, semi-arid ecosystem that receives less than 340 millimeters of rain annually. Water from its peaks trickles down porous rocks and underground channels to erupt into Amboseli's springs, giving birth to its marshes. But since 1912, Kilimanjaro has lost 80 percent of its snow and scientists fear the mountain will be iceless by 2033.
2. In 1991, Amboseli was declared a UNESCO man and biosphere reserve, thus involving the locals in biodiversity conservation and restricting their activities to specific zones. The park is a core zone for conservation, research, and education. Around it is a buffer zone for low-impact sustainable practices

like eco-tourism, and the land beyond is a transition zone for agriculture.

3. The Maasai never ate wildlife unless there was a severe draught, and their nomadic pastoralist lifestyle did not compete with wildlife. Even today, Amboseli is too small to support a herd of 200 elephants, which disperses to community lands during the rainy season. Amboseli's success relies on the zoning. Still, human-wildlife conflict occurs when predators kill livestock and elephants destroy farmland. Supporting the community helps both people and wildlife thrive.

4. Habitat in Amboseli is changing. The water table rose, increasing the soil salinity and destroying the woodlands. Thriving elephants de-barked and fell trees, thus changing the habitat, reducing some species and wiping out others. As community-owned land gets subdivided and fenced, and the number of people, houses, and livestock increases, the wildlife habitat shrinks and fragments, increasing human-wildlife conflict. In order to manage it, it is critical to:
    a. Enforce zoning plans and secure migratory corridors and critical dispersal areas for wildlife.
    b. Encourage wildlife-compatible land use practices like ecotourism and livestock production.
    c. Reimburse humans for loss of livestock killed by wildlife.

On our way home, we passed a large herd of impalas with multiple males — an unusual sight. Impala herds usually comprise many females with their youth and only one dominant male, but lone males gather into coalitions and challenge them for the herd.

"The dominant male lost the fight," Francis said.

He was right. Further down the road, a lone male walked alone to who knows where.

"What will happen to him?" I asked.

"He'll recover and come back to challenge them again. If he loses, he'll join another herd of lone males."

It was sad, even though I was glad the other males had their chance, and the females had a few males to choose from. But whether you are predator or prey, life in the savanna is ruthless. As ABBA used to sing, the winner takes it all.

"Look at those toothbrush bushes." Francis pointed to some bushes along the road. I studied them carefully. They had leaves, but I failed to see a single toothbrush.

"Toothbrush?"

"People cut the branches and chew on them to brush their teeth. It brightens your teeth and makes them healthy if you use them for a long time."

He must have been right, since almost everyone here has dazzling bright smiles — besides a few curmudgeons, most of them tourists.

We were almost out of the park when we met an industrious dung beetle. About two inches long, black and unassuming, he was laser-focused on rolling a dung ball along the road to some secret place.

"Where is he going?" I asked.

"He's looking for a moist place to bury it and deposit his eggs. Then, when they hatch, his babies will have something to feed on."

That must sound delicious if you happen to be a dung beetle, but I'll take a pass. As we watched, a second dung beetle came out of nowhere and planted himself on top of the dung ball.

"Is he trying to steal it?"

"No. He's here to help. He'll take over when the first one gets tired."

Beetle number one kept pushing as Beetle number two settled comfortably on the dung ball to get wheeled around with it. But unfortunately, since One pushed with his hind feet, he had no way to see where the dung ball went. But we did. Up, down, and sideways. Down in the ditch, back up, back down. He was making excellent time, but I didn't envy the dung-sitter one bit. I could just imagine how sick and dizzy he got, let alone getting concussed every time he hit the ground headfirst. But the brave beetles didn't give up. Two held on for dear life, while One kept valiantly pushing.

I'd have loved to see where they went, but it looked like it would take a while, so we left them to their travails and headed home. It's our last night at the Kimba Lodge in Amboseli. Tomorrow, we're driving to Tsavo, our last stop before heading home.

But for tonight, as a special treat, I booked a massage and a facial at the resort's spa, hoping to soothe the aches in my shoulders and the stiffness in my neck after getting rattled in Tank.

The massage was more vigorous than kind and very oily, and missed the sore spots that needed it most. I wanted to tell her to slow down a little, since she gets paid by the hour, so if she works slower, she works less, but she didn't look like she'd welcome my suggestions, so I kept my mouth shut. Funny how you know if people care just by the way they touch you. Sometimes you feel cared for, sometimes you're just a chore. For this young lady, I was just what stood between her and dinner.

The facial was pretty good though, with all sorts of

substances smelling like herbs, fruit, and flowers being spread on, then removed from my face. I got a bit worried when, in my naked oily state, she had me bend over a steaming bowl, but I was so cold that the steam felt good.

The last night's dinner highlight was a show from the crew. It was someone's birthday, so the entire staff — a couple dozen — gathered to sing and dance Hakuna Matata. They projected so much infectious joy it was hard to sit in your chair. The audience sang along, and many joined the dance in a fitting last night at Amboseli.

CHAPTER 42
ON DUNG BEETLES

I know it's silly to include a whole chapter on dung beetles alongside lions, elephants, and other majestic creatures, but I couldn't resist. But you can. If you don't care about either dung or beetles, skip it and move on.

As one might imagine, dung beetles are beetles that feed on feces. But if you think that's crappy, think again. Dung beetles belong to the sacred family of scarabs. In Ancient Egypt, they were revered as the divine manifestation of the morning sun, and they represented rebirth and resurrection, good luck, and fortune. Egyptians saw the dung balls the beetles rolled as a symbol of the sun rolling across the sky.

They believed the scarabs were males who reproduced by depositing their semen into a dung ball. This supposed self-creation mirrored that of Khepri, the god creating himself out of nothing.

But that's a bit passe. Let's get into here and now. What are dung beetles and why should you care?

Dung beetles are round-ish, with short elytra (wing covers) exposing the end of their abdomen. They are usually dark with a metallic sheen, and they're seldom bigger than an inch and a half. Some males have a curved horn on their head, and they are called — you guessed it — rhinoceros beetles.

Dung beetles are mighty. They can roll dung balls ten times heavier than themselves. The horned dung beetle, in particular, holds the title of the strongest insect in the world. He can pull 1,141 times his body weight — equivalent to you pulling six double-decker buses.

They can bury 250 times their weight of dung in one night, and eat more dung than their weight in 24 hours, more than some politicians. But, unlike politicians, dung beetles are beneficial to the environment by converting manure into nutrients.

They operate in various ways. Rollers roll dung into round balls they use as food or for breeding. Tunnelers bury dung in their elaborate burrows extending several feet underground, sometimes with multiple chambers, each containing its own dung ball. Dwellers just live inside the dung to enjoy the cozy intimacy.

Dung beetles live just about everywhere on earth except Antarctica. You can find them in the desert, the savanna, the farmlands, and the forests, but they don't like extreme cold or dryness.

Dung beetles will eat the dung of herbivores, but they prefer that of omnivores. They will also feed on decaying vegetal matter, and some of them even prey on millipedes and insects. Interestingly, dung beetles do not need to eat or drink anything else, because the dung provides them with all the nutrients they need. Just let that sink in!

Most dung beetles look for dung by smell, but some are craftier. They attach themselves to the business parts of their preferred dung producer and wait for the dung delivery. After capturing it, they fashion it into a ball and roll it away, following a straight-ish line towards their target.

If you think that's easy, since nobody needs that crap, think again. Other dung beetles will try to steal the precious commodity from its rightful owner, so the creator must roll his treasure away and hide it as fast as he can. Fortunately, dung beetles are not only mighty but skillful. They navigate by the Milky Way, the first known creatures besides humans to use the galaxy for orientation. They use the moon's polarized light and the brightness of the stars to roll their dung balls in a straight line.

The male and female "rollers" work together to roll and bury a dung ball that they turn into a brooding ball. The male usually rolls the ball while the female hitchhikes or follows, helping when the going gets tough.

When they find the perfect place for their family, which is usually a soft, moist, well-hidden spot, they bury the dung ball, then mate underground. Once romance is over, they prepare the brooding ball with all the amenities before the female lays her eggs inside. Some leave it afterwards, but others stay to guard their offspring as they go through metamorphosis.

So that's who dung beetles are. But why should you care?

Dung beetles are important for agriculture because they speed up nutrient recycling and improve soil structure. They have been shown to improve plant growth on rehabilitated coal mines and spread the seeds from animal dung. They also protect livestock from disease by removing the dung, which is a breeding ground for flies. That's why some countries introduced them to fields to improve animal husbandry. Dung beetles save the United States cattle industry $380 million annually through burying manure, as per the American Institute of Biological Sciences.

In Australia, introducing 23 species of imported dung beetles improved the quality and fertility of cattle pastures and reduced Australian bush flies by 90 percent. Dung beetles were even trialed on Sydney beaches to manage dog droppings.

New Zealand is now looking at importing dung beetles to improve their pastures. They hope to reduce agricultural greenhouse gas emissions by incorporating manure into the soil without using machines. In South America, African dung beetles were introduced to control livestock diseases.

See? I told you that dung beetles weren't crappy.

CHAPTER 43
HEADING TO TSAVO

Day eleven of thirteen is upon us, and it's time to think about going home. The last day when we leave Tsavo West to drive to the Nairobi Airport for an almost midnight flight, is still in debate. Our safari itinerary says we get dropped off at the airport in the late afternoon, but what do we do before that? And what's late afternoon?

"It's six. Seven is early evening, so six is late afternoon," I said. Steve, like he always does, disagreed.

"It's four. Six is early evening."

"Seriously? Four is early afternoon," I said.

"Nope. That's one, and two."

We bickered for a while, but it really doesn't matter what we think. What matters is what Francis decides it is, and that gets me to my point: Boys and girls, read your contract carefully before you pay. Every little word of it. And remember, no matter how smart you think you are, you're likely doing this for the first time, while the other party does it for a living.

Either way, whether it's six or four, it's still too early for a flight departing at midnight. We'll have to talk to Francis. But in the meantime, we'll be heading to Tsavo West.

Tsavo West is one of Kenya's largest national parks, and it was even bigger before it got divided from Tsavo East, which is larger still. The trip from Amboseli looked tricky. If the weather looked good — as in no more rain — we would take the magic shortcut, crossing some river whose bridge got washed out by the rains, and get there in two hours. If not, we'd take the long way around, which would take twice as long.

We took the shortcut, but it still took four hours on some of the worst roads of our trip. It had potholes on top of potholes, and more dust than I cared to inhale. We passed by women carrying babies and baskets and buckets and bundles of firewood, and men carrying sticks. We skirted cows and goats and a vast flock of sheep guarded not by dogs but by a large ram wearing a sturdy plastic apron.

"Maasai family planning," Francis said. "When they want no babies, they'll put that thing on the ram so he can no longer mount the sheep."

It may not be obvious, since it rains every day, but it turns out that we're in the dry season. Normally, the grass would be scarce, so sheep wouldn't have enough milk to feed the young lambs. Rather than suffer that waste, the sheep herders outfitted the ram with a contraceptive apron.

"They do that with goats, too."

"How about cows?"

"I never saw that done with cows," Francis said pensively.

"Of course not. Who'd dare put that on a bull?" Steve said.

We passed what looked like a shipping container labeled "Regional Trauma Center," in large black letters, and I felt grateful that none of us was sick. It wasn't the first health facility I had seen, and this one looked better than most, but getting sick here looked like a lousy idea. We skirted an informal market and got chased by a young vendor intent on selling us some fruit, whether or not we wanted them. We waved at a kid offering us a tiny puppy, then the humans thinned, and we passed by fields of sunflowers following the scorching sun. Across from them there were large fields of corn they call maize, which is Kenya's staple food.

"I thought Maasai didn't work the land," I said.

"They don't. They just graze cows. They rent this land to the Kikuyu, who work it."

Tribe business is very complicated in Kenya. Maasai are herders and guards, Kikuyu are entrepreneurs, Camba are hunters and preachers, Kalenjin are runners, and there are thirty more that I forgot. Their cultures and languages differ, but most can speak Swahili and English. They live in different regions of Kenya, but they mix in big cities.

The cultivated fields disappeared, and we got back to the scrub with scattered thorny acacia that only elephants and giraffes can love.

"Animals are different in Tsavo," Francis said.

"How so?"

"They are afraid of people, and elephants here are very aggressive."

"Why?"

"We are in Camba land. Remember, I told you that Camba people used to be hunters? They still are. Even now, there are plenty of poachers who kill elephants for their tusks and leopards for their skin."

"How do they kill them?"

"With their bow and arrows."

"Can you kill an elephant with bow and arrows?"

"Yes. With poison. They poison their arrows with a powerful poison they concoct from tree bark. A band of them all go after the same animal. They know where to aim to hit an organ or a blood vessel."

"How long does it take it to die?"

"Minutes. Then they cut the skin and remove the tusks to sell."

"What sort of poison do they use?"

Francis shrugged, but I looked it up: It's the natural Acokanthera poison which is easily extracted from the sap of Acokanthera oppositifolia, a.k.a. the bushman poison bush, a plant that contains cardiac glycosides, heart toxins strong enough to kill humans, and apparently elephants.

"Don't they get caught?"

"Some do. But it's not easy. I had a neighbor who did it. He tried to sell me a leopard skin, and I asked him where he got it. He laughed."

"Did you report him?"

"I didn't. See, if I went to the authorities, they'd want proof, and I had none. They'd want me to be a witness, and if they bring the man in and find nothing, they'll let him go. And if he can kill a leopard, he surely can kill me. Even if they put him in jail, his family and cousins would come after me. The only way to elude them would be to go to jail too, and not just for a day or two. For a long time."

"What happened to the man?"

"He disappeared. One night he didn't come back. Some say he went to Tanzania, but I think the elephants got him."

The landscape changed again as we reached the lava fields of Mt Sheitani, the Devil's Mountain, which blasted out its insides a few hundred years ago, covering the earth with jagged, porous black lava rock that is still bare after all this time. The two-hour trip had turned into four by the time we made it to the Kilaguni Serena Lodge, our last stop on this trip. We were greeted, as always, with a wet towel to clean the red dust off our hands and faces and a cold mango juice to soothe our parched throats. After a quick check-in, two men grabbed our luggage and took us to our room.

It was a lovely room with a gigantic bed with mosquito nets, a beautiful view of the park, electricity, hot water, and internet! What a treat! Add to that the chameleon on the porch. Our new pet turned out to miss a paw and have a broken tail, but that didn't bother him one bit.

Lunch was great too — Osso Bucco with mashed potatoes and a splendid view over a local waterhole where two buffaloes enjoyed a mud spa, a few nostalgic marabou storks looking like unemployed funeral directors eyed the waterhole for frogs, and a couple of gazelles grazed the green grass. It was an idyllic landscape we won't soon forget.

We rested for an hour, then headed out for our first Tsavo game drive.

CHAPTER 44
KENYAN FOOD

I'M NOT sure how much of the food on our safari was authentic Kenyan, and how much of it had been adapted to our delicate western palate. But Kenyan food is rich in beans, vegetables, and cereal, especially corn. Curries and chapatis, which are common, show a significant Indian influence. Fresh fruit is always available, but cheese is rare and usually imported. Desserts are more of an afterthought. Here are a few of the most common dishes:

1. *Ugali.* Corn, which they call maize, is to Kenyans what rice is to Japanese, potatoes to Irish, and bread to Romanians: it's Kenya's staple food. Ground white maize gets boiled into ugali, a thick polenta they serve with greens, beans, stew, or whatever is dinner. Ugali is eaten with your hands, and it's not a looker. It's bland, heavy, and moist, and it borrows the aroma of whatever it's served with.
2. *Chapati.* A flatbread of Indian origin. Flour dough gets rolled into a circle, then fried in oil until crispy on the edges. It' served with curries and stews.

3. *Githeri.* A traditional Kikuyu dish. It's a hearty mix of beans and corn boiled with onions and tomatoes and maybe a few chilies to give it a bit of heat. Regional variations may include garlic, cumin, turmeric, or coconut milk. Goes well with chapatis.
4. *Sukuma Wiki,* meaning "stretch the week" in Swahili, is a side dish of sautéed collard greens or kale. It's served with ugali.
5. *Matoke* is a plantain stew. Plantains get sautéed with potatoes, tomatoes, onions, garlic, and chilies until they soften. Somewhat. Served with rice, ugali, or a chapati.
6. *Pilau.* Rice cooked with cumin, cardamon, cinnamon, and cloves. Goes well with meat stew and fresh tomatoes.
7. *Chai.* Though Kenya produces excellent coffee, tea is many locals' drink of choice. They brew it dark, mix it with milk, and sweeten it with lots of sugar, but it still makes you pucker.
8. *Mandazi.* A sweet, deep-fried, doughnut-like snack flavored with cardamom or nutmeg usually served for breakfast.
9. *Mutura.* That's Kenyan sausage made from a mixture of meat, offal, blood, and spices, grilled and eaten as street food.
10. Stews made from vegetables like carrots, peppers, peas, or potatoes in a tomato sauce with onions and maybe some meat. They get flavored with a *mchuzi* mix — a mixture of garlic, paprika, turmeric, coriander, cumin, fennel, and corn flour.
11. *Nyama Choma.* Kenya's answer to barbecue, often advertised on the buildings by the side of the road. It's usually goat, beef, or mutton. The fat and the

grizzle are the choice parts, and the only flavoring is salt. Beef is common — no wonder, with all those cows — but chicken is a treat, and it's expensive.

"If you take a girl out," Francis said, "you want to buy her chicken. She'll tell all her friends, and they'll say 'Oh, so-and-so is such a good boy.'"
"How about beef?"
Francis shook his head.
"No beef. They'll think you're no good."
Not that surprising, I might add. Kenyan beef bears little resemblance to the juicy, melt-in-your-mouth steaks you might be used to. As one would expect from the Kenyan outdoorsy cows who spend their lives chewing on spiny bushes and trampling each other for a blade of grass. No wonder Kenyan beef is so muscular that it resists chewing. It also resists cutting with the blunt knives we'd been given, so Steve gave it up after the first day. I didn't. I was perpetually hungry, since our meals were always late, but that beef required lots of determination and good dentures.

Most safari places serve breakfast from 6:30 to 8:30, lunch from 12:30 to 2:30, and dinner from 7:30 to nine. Your safari will revolve around the meal schedule, but your guide can request a boxed lunch or breakfast if needed. Most meals are a self-serve buffet with occasional carving stations or eggs and pancakes made to order. Restaurants have bars serving alcoholic and nonalcoholic drinks, including water. Prices are around 3 dollars for a small bottle of water, 4–5 dollars for a beer and 6–7 dollars for a cocktail.

Breakfast consists of pastries, cereal, juices, and fruit. There's also bacon and sausage and an egg-cooking station, and bread for toasting, but bread is not their strength. Coffee is brought at the table, and it's usually instant, despite coffee being one of Kenya's major crops.

Lunch is soup, often served at the table, and one to two meats, usually in a stew, or grilled fish, plus a few sides: Lyonnaise potatoes, mashed potatoes, sweet potatoes, or rice plus sautéed vegetables, like carrots and peas, and frequently a few flavorful Indian dishes.

Dinner is very much like lunch, with beef stew, baked fish, and side dishes. There once was a carving station with rump steak — that was a challenge. There's always fruit, sometimes cheese, and desserts: cakes and steamed puddings — bread pudding, vanilla pudding — with custard sauce.

The food is plentiful and mostly good. Some is delicious, some OK, some edible, but I certainly ate more than I should have. Still, I found the Tripadvisor reviews overstated. I eat my own cooking more often than I'd like, and it's not spectacular, but I am a foodie. I've eaten all over the world — with abandon, I should say. We spent months in France, Italy, and Japan, and we live in Thailand, which is all about food — delicious, fresh, and so spicy it makes you cry. Kenyan food is not like that.

But we didn't go there for the food, and neither should you. We went to see wildlife, learn about Africa, and maybe even learn a bit about ourselves.

CHAPTER 45
TSAVO

Francis was right. Things are different in Tsavo. Gone are the endless plains covered in undulating golden grasses; gone are the gazelles, the giraffes, and the elephants blocking the road. Everything here is hills and mountains covered in thick green brush and massive umbrella-like trees with no animal in sight.

They do have butterflies — today looks like butterfly day, with hundreds of them dancing around every tree, lending it magic. Most are white, with a few yellow and red who must be lost and looking for their tribes. Butterflies don't live long, you know. Sometimes only a day, so they must do whatever it takes to meet the love of their life and get down to business.

We also met a bunch of birds. Couples of guinea fowls, with their polka-dotted gray plumage and the silly little crowns on their blue heads, stubbornly refusing to give way. They ran and ran ahead of the car until their short skinny legs got tired, then flew away. The female would sometimes veer off, but the male stayed to fight, puffing himself into a threatening stance, without noticing he was smaller than our wheel. His harsh alarm blared like a Russian curse coming out of a rusty speaker rather than a bird's throat.

Flocks of yellow-necked spurfowls, their naked, bright-yellow necks set off by their gray spotted plumage, stood in the road, scratching the red clay in search of termites for breakfast. When they saw us coming, they lifted their beaks to the sky to call a hoarse warning, clanging like they gargled on nails.

A white-bellied go-away bird (crinifer leucogaster) gave us the stink eye from a treetop, then told everyone who wanted to know that we were there, and we stank, in grumpy yelps sounding like someone with a nasty cold telling you to get lost.

No animals seemed to be around until we met the jackals. We'd already seen a few loners, looking just like dogs with their long muzzles, sharp ears, and fluffy tails. But this time there were six of them, holding a convention in the middle of the road until we rudely interrupted and set them running down the road to shake us off.

But unlike them, who could have turned left or right into the scrub anytime, we had nowhere else to go, so we kept following them down the road. Three of them eventually had enough and ran off, but the others kept running, glancing back every once in a while to check if we were still there. We were.

The other three reappeared behind us and followed to see what we were up to. Just going about our business, I wanted to say, but with Tank dropping in and out of potholes, I worried I'd cut off my tongue.

The first three kept running like they'd never stop. The ones behind us got closer. Soon enough, we were surrounded.

"I thought the jackals were loners. Is this a pack?"

"Most likely a litter of almost grown cubs," Francis said, struggling to pass them without running them over. "They usually live in pairs."

Like hyenas and civets, jackals are opportunistic predators who scavenge or hunt small mammals, birds, and reptiles. Their large paws allow them to run long-distance at speeds of up to

10 mph, and they are most active at dawn and dusk. They live in monogamous pairs which mark their territory with urine and feces, but young adults may stay with their parents until they establish their own territories.

We finally passed the jackals and checked a few waterholes — all empty — then scoured the potholed roads up and down, but found nothing more.

"Whoever comes for a safari and only visits Tsavo, they'll be disappointed this year," Francis said. "They won't see much."

He was right. We've fortunately seen a lot at the other parks, especially in the North, but both Tsavo and Amboseli were a bit of a letdown as far as animals go. The lodgings were great, the food good, and the service mostly excellent, but if seeing animals is what you want to do, you'd better hedge your bets by planning to visit a few different places.

Oh, well. We'll have more luck on the evening drive, I thought. But, as it often happens, life had other plans. Steve's quick power nap turned into an hour, then two. He woke up flushed and shivering. He had no pain, no diarrhea, no trouble breathing, but he went back to sleep instead of coming to lunch, and that's when I knew for sure that something wasn't right.

We're at Tsavo West, five hours away from Nairobi, and we're flying out tomorrow at midnight, but we have to check out of here before 10 a.m. What do I do with a sick Steve for 14 hours without a room? What do I do with him for two days on the road?

I'd better get him well. I fed him the cake I'd absconded from the lunch buffet — not the best food for a sick person, but that's all I could get him to eat. He's been known to live on cookies and candy when I wasn't around. I forced him to drink glass after glass of water, then tea, then more water. I fed him some Motrin and put him back to bed.

The afternoon drive was out of the question, so I went to tell Francis, who was waiting in the parking lot.

Everyone else was heading out for their evening drive, hopeful and eager, with their sunglasses, cameras, and binoculars. I must confess I was half envious and half sad to miss our last game drive. But it is what it is. I was lucky to see what I'd seen.

Francis was concerned to hear about Steve.

"Did you tell the people at the reception?"

"No."

"You should."

"What for?"

"They'll get you in touch with the clinic."

I shivered. I remembered the Regional Trauma Center in the shipping container, so I wasn't one bit curious about the clinic.

"I'll manage. For the moment, I have everything I need. If I need more, I'll ask."

He seemed doubtful, but agreed to come see if we can get a late checkout and keep our room until after lunch. Still, it was not that simple. Staying late would mean we had to pay another daily park fee for each of us and the car, since our permit to be in the park expired at 10.

But there was no late checkout. The place was fully booked, so, sick or not, we had to leave. Where? Anywhere.

Grateful for the internet, I got on my computer and, after a few failed attempts, I booked us a room at an airport hotel. That would give us a place to rest between, say, 2 p.m. when we arrive in Nairobi, and 10 p.m. when we need to check in for our flight. We'll have a bed, a bathroom, and hopefully even internet. Then we'll board the plane to Bangkok, where we have to change planes again, but I won't worry about that right now. We'll cross that bridge when we get to it.

Fortunately, our lovely room with a view of the park made

up for our missed game drive. Chameleons chased each other on the porch, rolling their bulging round eyes to keep us in view. A dazzle of zebras stopped to graze straight ahead, presenting their shapely stripped bottoms and swishing their tails to smack the flies.

By now, Steve had also developed diarrhea — quite possibly thanks to the cake I fed him. So I gave him Imodium, more liquids, and then more cake for dinner, so he can take more Motrin. Don't judge me, please. I'm not impressed with myself either, but I'm doing the best that I can.

CHAPTER 46
THE LAST DAY

IT'S ALMOST 5 a.m. as I write this. It's still dark, and we're leaving at nine. And guess who's got an awful diarrhea? No, not Steve.

Thankfully, I'd refreshed my Imodium supplies at a Narok chemist — that's what they call pharmacies here — because I've been eating it like candy. I also packed a roll of toilet paper and some moist cleaning towelettes.

The plan is to stay flexible. If we're looking OK by the time we reach Nairobi, we'll go to see Kenya's National Museum and the popular Karen Blixen Museum. It's the old farm of a famous Danish writer who wrote *Out of Africa,* a book made into a popular movie with Robert Redford and Meryl Streep. Worth watching, if you have the time. Her old home is now a museum showcasing life in colonial Kenya.

If we're having trouble, Francis will drop us at the airport hotel for the eight hours before our flight. But, after missing the last two game drives, I really hope we make it to the museum.

That was the plan this morning.

But, of course, Steve didn't feel well, so he slept in the back for most of the trip, then started vomiting. We have no plastic bags, since they are not allowed in Kenya, and the paper bag I gave him leaked all over him and the car, making a terrible mess. We stopped by the side of the road to clean him up under Francis's worried eyes.

"Should we go to the hospital?" he asked.

I shivered.

"No. But we'll skip the museum and go to the hotel," I said.

He looked doubtful, but I was determined, so a few hours later he dropped us at the Kozi Hotel, a small hotel with clean, cozy rooms, decent Wi-Fi, and a shuttle that would take us to the airport in the evening.

Parting with Francis was hard. For two weeks, he was our guide, our driver, and our trusted companion. We chatted, we laughed, and we learned from each other. We couldn't have hoped for a better person to introduce us to Kenya, and we were deeply grateful.

But friendship is friendship, and business is business. We gave him an envelope with a good tip in dollars, plus all the Kenyan money we had left, keeping just enough for emergencies. Before leaving, he called George — remember George? The company owner, who had organized our whole itinerary? And had me speak to him.

I thanked George profusely for everything, especially for assigning us Francis. I promised a stellar review on Tripadvisor, and I asked his permission to use his name in this book (I had already asked Francis.)

He said yes, but it took twenty minutes. He's a charmer, but not a man of few words, George.

Our trip home was long and exhausting, but uneventful, other than the Nairobi airport having more security checks than any other airport I can remember, and people who could not care less about queuing. They cut in front of us everywhere, from the security lines and passport control to the toilets. By the time we finally boarded the plane, all we wanted was to be out of there.

But our flight made it back in time. After another short flight and a short taxi ride, we were home, delighted to be back.

It was a wonderful safari, and I'm glad we did it. We saw, experienced, and learned so much. But boy, does it feel good to be home and make your own schedule. To have power, hot water, and Wi-Fi. True, the fridge is empty and there's nobody to cook, clean, and do the dishes, but it's still great to be home.

CHAPTER 47
ONE YEAR LATER

OUR UPDATES:

It took us forever to recover after the Kenyan safari. Weeks later, our insides were still jittery, and we were still exhausted. We never had a fever, so it wasn't malaria, but I'm still not sure whether we ate or drank something fishy and caught some bug, or if we suffered from the side effects of the antimalarial medications. Or maybe it was just the jet lag, which gets so much worse as you get older. Still, a month later, we had recovered enough to be planning new travels. We took a cruise on the Mekong River through Vietnam and Cambodia, a one-week cruise in the Galapagos to fraternize with the seals and the fishes, and spent a long month crossing Europe from London to Bucharest, before returning to Thailand again.

Kenya updates:

Kenya's doctors and pharmacists went on strike for almost two months for unpaid salaries and unsuitable working conditions, leaving many patients with no medical care.

Youth-led demonstrators stormed the Kenyan Parliament to protest increasing taxes on essential goods. After multiple fatalities, the president withdrew the tax increase and dismissed the government, promising to address the economic challenges and fight corruption.

The Kenyan government launched a plan to eliminate FGM by 2030. The cornerstones are education, stricter enforcement of existing anti-FGM laws, establishing alternative rites of passage, and encouraging male advocacy. Still, some girls are taken abroad for the procedure. FGM performed by healthcare professionals led to a false sense of safety of the practice.

National Parks:

Severe floods led to hundreds of deaths and population displacement, damaging the infrastructure, agriculture, and tourism. The Mara bridge we crossed with Davis was washed away. National parks' entry fees increased several-fold.

Tsavo West launched a rhino ear-notching and transmitter fitting program to enhance rhinos tracking and protection. Twenty-one black rhinos were translocated to restore rhino populations affected by poaching. Fifty elephants from the overpopulated Mwea National Reserve were relocated to the Aberdare National Park.

The Maasai:

The Maasai continue to face challenges. Their land rights are threatened, especially in Tanzania, where the government is accused of relocating the Maasai from the Ngorongoro Conservation Area by using force, arbitrary arrests, and cutting healthcare and education subsidies. Maasai's relocation disrupted their traditional lifestyle, leading to economic hardships and social disintegration.

A controversial small study published in September 2024 suggesting that cattle and wildlife can coexist challenged the policies restricting cattle grazing in protected areas and rekindled the debate on the Maasai's role in conservation.

Conservation efforts:

Lions: Kenya's lion population was estimated at 2,589 individuals in 2023, a 25 percent increase over the past five years, showing successful conservation initiatives.

Cheetahs: The 2021 wildlife census estimated 1,160 cheetahs living in Kenya. The Mara Predator Conservation Program shows a deceptive increase by five individuals in the Mara cheetah population between 2022 and 2023. Why deceptive? Because the study area was expanded and the female-to-male sex ratio has declined, which means fewer adult females can contribute to population growth.

Leopards: Limited data from camera trap surveys shows stable populations in protected areas.

Elephants: Thanks to habitat conservation efforts, Kenya's elephant population increased from 16,000 to 34,000 between 1989 and 2023.

The Northern White Rhinos:

Remember our old friends Najin and Fatu, the last two female northern rhinos at Ol Pejeta? Here's the latest update, as per CNN:

"The project successfully impregnated a southern white rhino via IVF, creating a path for restoring the northern white rhino species.

The impregnation was an international effort. The sperm was collected from a southern white rhinoceros named Athos, who lives at Zoo Salzburg in Austria. The egg cells were retrieved from Elenore, a southern white rhinoceros living in the Pairi Daiza Zoo in Belgium. The samples were then transferred to Italy and fertilized in vitro.

Two embryos were transferred to Kenya and implanted in a surrogate mother named Curra at the Ol Pejeta Conservancy in September 2023. The process of implanting the embryos included using a male "teaser" bull, named Ouwan, to simulate typical mating behaviors.

Unfortunately, both Curra and Ouwan were found dead in

November. It's believed the pair fell ill due to a severe bacterial infection following heavy climate change–related rains, which flooded the surrogate enclosure.

Curra was pregnant with a 70-day-old male fetus. Tissue taken from the fetus confirmed that the pregnancy was the result of the embryo transfer.

The next step of the program will be to select a new southern white rhino surrogate mother and teaser bull, then develop a northern white rhino embryo to implant in the surrogate."

CHAPTER 48
FINAL THOUGHTS

OUR SAFARI WAS AN AMAZING EXPERIENCE. It opened our eyes and our hearts to things and people we knew little about. It was fun, exhilarating, educational, worrisome, and, at times, very sad.

Kenya, like the rest of the world, is changing fast. It's a young country with an average age of nineteen, and it's growing. It's evolving from its traditional ways and modernizing its economy, its infrastructure, and its expectations towards the 21st century.

That requires more crops, more roads, more cars, more houses. It's unavoidable that more and more of the land that is now home to wildlife and pastoralists will be cultivated in the name of progress.

It's not easy. People struggle, torn between their traditions and the pressure of a new society. But they change.

Animals can't. The lions, the elephants, and the cheetahs have no place to go. Their numbers diminish because of habitat loss and fragmentation, the rhythm of their lives is impacted by climate change, and their contacts with humans — whether it's the farmers killing them to safeguard their crops, the Maasai hunting them to protect their cows, or the poachers killing them for money — are all nefarious.

The conservation efforts are amazing. From the rangers looking after the last northern white rhinos, to the vets trying to save the dart-poisoned elephants and the conservationists helping the locals establish bee fences to deter elephants from raiding their crops, so many people work hard to help the animals survive. That's difficult, and I'm not overoptimistic, but maintaining them is cheaper, easier, and more likely to succeed than trying to reintroduce them once they are extinct. Despite titanic efforts and massive costs, most reintroduction efforts fail. Why?

Reintroductions depend on many factors: habitat suitability, food availability, the season of release and type of release (soft, as in supervised and gradual versus hard, as in just let go), and the origin of the source population (wild-caught versus captive-born).

Reintroduction projects are carried out because populations are declining, so they often use captive-born individuals. But these animals are not used to the wild. They don't know how to hunt, hide, socialize, breed, and nest like their wild counterparts. They lack immunity to the local diseases. Even worse, they're not afraid of humans, which is a life-saving skill when you're wild.

So, if reintroduction is seldom successful, what can we do to help?

Good question. I had been of two minds about going on safari at first, but now I know it makes a big difference. Your money will help those working in the tourist industry and their families. Your presence will show them that these animals are important, and they are worth more to them alive than dead.

That worked with the Maasai. When they saw that

preserving wildlife is more lucrative than hunting it, the hunters turned into guardians.

So, going on a safari might help. But if going on a safari is not for you but you still want to help, consider contributing your time or your money to wildlife funds. Fundraise, whether you run a marathon or ask for donations for your birthday. Educate yourself, then others — it's interesting and fun, and it multiplies your reach.

The easiest thing you can do — cheaper, too — is to live greener and avoid waste in whichever way works for you. Every bit helps, whether it's walking more and driving less, growing wildflowers for the bees instead of mowing the lawn, reusing plastic bottles, or turning up the AC thermostat.

Teach your children to do the same. Just think: Today's children will probably never see a northern white rhino. But if we do nothing, their children might never see a cheetah, a turtle, or an elephant. How sad is that?

As for Steve and I, we're planning our next adventure. Where will it take us? We don't yet know. But wherever we go, we'll do our best to keep an open mind, learn, and have a positive impact on the place and the people.

APPENDIX 1 — REFERENCES

What to watch and read before you go, and maybe even if you don't.

Movies:

***** **Africa, a documentary** by the BBC with David Attenborough. Wonderful to watch with the whole family, even if you don't plan a safari. It has an amazing filmography, great stories, and David Attenborough's excellent narration: poignant, witty, and often hilarious. Six episodes took four years to produce, and you'll understand why when you see the last one. We found it on Amazon.

***** **David Attenborough Planet Earth: Giraffes, Africa's Gentle Giants** BBC. An amazing one hour show about giraffes and the people trying to help them.

**** **Giraffes, the Forgotten Giants**. A documentary by PBS. An excellent 50 minutes movie about the peculiarities of giraffes.

***** **The Insane Biology of the Spotted Hyena** by Real Science. Excellent documentary about what makes hyenas such fearsome predators.

**** **The Leopardess: Haunted Huntress** by Get Factual.

An excellent one-hour documentary on the life of the elusive leopards in the Serengeti.

***** **Punda, the Zebra - the Tale of an Unusual hero**. The touching story of a baby zebra growing up to become a stallion.

***** **The Last Lion of Liuwa Plain**. The emotional, first-person story of the only survivor of her pride.

Books:

**** **Africa Safari Chronicles: Kenya**, by Leo M. Cyr and Beth M. Cyr. Very informative for choosing the right safari, what to pack, what to expect. It's short but useful.

**** **Fodor's Complete Guide to African Safaris**. Lots of useful info on where and when to go, how to prepare and what to expect.

*** **Images of Africa: A Couple's Comical Safari Saga**. This is a memoir written by a couple on safari, and it's an informative, easy read, though it gets a bit scary at times. Apparently tipping in the savanna is just slightly more expensive than in Times Square, but the roads are even worse than in Upstate NY. Go figure!

*** **Safari Ants, Baggy Pants and Elephant**s by Susie Kelly. A loving memoir of Kenya written by someone who grew up there.

Web Resources:

For everything: Wikipedia — the source of all knowledge.

Maasai association: https://maasai-association.org/ceremonies.html#:~:text=There%20are%20many%20ceremonies%20in,junior%20elder%20ceremony)%2C%20etc.

Hyena birth magic: https://africageographic.com/stories/hyena-birth-moment-magic/#2

The ugly five: https://www.lionworldtravel.com/news/ugly-five-animals-africa

Appendix 1 — References

Animal mating habits: https://www.bbcearth.com/news/mind-blowing-animal-mating-habits#

Carnivores reintroduction to the wild: https://www.sciencedirect.com/science/article/abs/pii/S0006320707004417?casa_token=u1wBLYMX4KYAAAAA:NvKHiR7psjI2drY0iiDRO_84dPKK_IlJkSTdEu9hhtA5s0B6KoAabT_6NKm5EY5SKvB0AGMSc9Q

The wolf needs more training: https://wilderness-society.org/the-wolf-needs-more-training/\

APPENDIX 2 — WHAT YOU CAN DO TO SUPPORT CONSERVATION

1. Reduce, Reuse, and Recycle. Less waste means less pollution and habitat destruction. It's cheaper, too. Shopping for second-hand clothes at charity shops can be just as much fun as going to the mall, but way easier on the wallet.
2. Support Conservation Organization such as the World Wildlife Fund (WWF), The Nature Conservancy, and Rainforest Trust through donations, memberships, or volunteering. They have online opportunities if you can't travel far.
3. Cut down on meat and buy local produce to stay healthier and avoid industrial farming, which harms the environment.
4. Reduce water use to protect freshwater ecosystems and reduce the strain on water resources. Fixing leaks and turning off taps will also reduce your water bills.
5. Avoid palm oil, soy, and other products tied to deforestation. Look for certifications like Rainforest Alliance or Fair Trade.

Appendix 2 — What You Can Do To Support Conservation

6. Walking, biking, and using public transport are healthier, cheaper, and more fun and they help reduce climate change.
7. Reduce your energy bills: turn off lights, buy energy-efficient appliances, and opt for renewable energy.
8. Avoid wildlife products and exploitative animal tourism to reduce illegal wildlife trade and exploitation. When traveling, choose tourism operators prioritizing wildlife conservation.
9. Plant native trees to help restore habitats, increase biodiversity and absorb carbon dioxide.
10. Talk to friends and family, share on social media, and advocate for environmental policies.
11. Take part in projects like INaturalist and eBird to track animal populations, monitor habitats, or report sightings.
12. Turn your yard into a wildlife shelter: plant native species instead of a lawn and install birdhouses and insect hotels.
13. Buy shade-grown coffee and sustainably sourced cocoa to help preserve wildlife habitats, especially for migratory birds.
14. Minimize outdoor lighting to reduce light pollution. Nocturnal light disrupts birds, bats, and insects and interferes with their natural migration and feeding patterns.
15. Contain your pets to protect local wildlife. Don't abandon them into the wild and let them harm the environment, like the Burmese pythons in the Florida Everglades and the rabbits in Australia.
16. Avoid herbicides and pesticides that can harm wildlife, pollinators, and you. DDT, used to control

Appendix 2 — What You Can Do To Support Conservation

malaria-carrying mosquitoes, damaged bald eagles and peregrine falcons by thinning their eggshells. It also caused health problems in humans. Insecticides harm the navigation, reproduction, and immune systems of bees and contribute to their massive decline. Roundup is linked to cancers. Avoid them.
17. Support legislation meant to safeguard endangered species, limit habitat destruction, and promote conservation.

AFTERWORD

Dear Reader,

I'm so glad you joined us on our safari. If you loved *Exploring Kenya*, **please leave a review** to help other readers find it. It means a lot to me.

Exploring Kenya is my love letter to the majestic lions, brave hyenas, industrious dung beetles, and the other inhabitants of the ever shrinking savanna. Watching them taught me a lot, touched my heart, and made me long to change their world for the better. But nobody can do it alone.

Still, I tried. I hope this book made you laugh, taught you a little, and made you care a lot. Did it?

Rada

Exploring Kenya review

ABOUT THE AUTHOR

Rada was born in Transylvania, ten miles from Dracula's Castle. Growing up between communists and vampires taught her that humans are fickle, but you can always trust dogs and books. That's why she read every book she could get, including the phone book (too many characters, not enough action), and adopted every stray she found, from dogs to frogs.

After joining her American husband, she spent years studying medicine and working in the ER, but she still speaks like Dracula's cousin.

Rada, her husband Steve, and their dog Guinness live in a cozy Adirondack cabin. They spend their days writing, hiking, and dreaming about traveling to faraway places.

facebook.com/RadaJonesMD
bookbub.com/profile/rada-jones

OTHER BOOKS BY RADA JONES

BECOMING K-9: A Bomb Dog's Memoir
BIONIC BUTTER: A Three-Pawed K-9 Hero
K-9 VIPER: The Veteran's Story
LOVELY K-9: A Prison Puppy
K-9 RAMBO: The Dutch Master
K-9 PROZAK: POW
K-9 HEROES: Final Mission
K-9 HEROES (BOOKS 1,2,3)
MORE K-9 HEROES (BOOKS 4,5,6)
MOM: A Dog Story Prequel to BECOMING K-9
RANGER: The Escape Artist

OVERDOSE: An ER Psychological Thriller
MERCY: An ER Thriller
POISON: An ER Thriller
DO HARM: A Cruise Thriller
SEE EVIL: A Cruise Thriller
TAKE LIVES: A Cruise Thriller
ER CRIMES: The Steele Files
Box Set: Books 1-3

STAY AWAY FROM MY ER, and Other Fun Bits of Wisdom

DRIVING ITALY: A Cheeky Travel Memoir
EXPLORING KENYA: A Cheeky Safari Memoir

Printed in Great Britain
by Amazon